POSTCARDS from WORLD WAR II

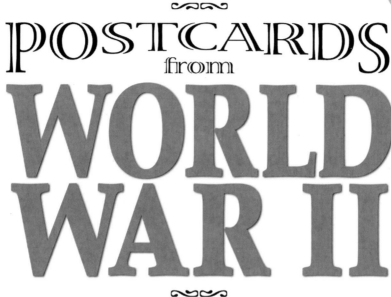

Robynn Clairday and Matt Clairday

SQUAREONE PUBLISHERS

Cover Design: Phaedra Mastrocola
In-House Editing: Marie Caratozzolo
Consultant: George J. Lankevich
Interior Design: Phaedra Mastrocola
Typesetting: Gary A. Rosenberg

Square One Publishers | Garden City Park, NY 11040 | **516-535-2010** | www.squareonepublishers.com

Library of Congress Cataloging-in-Publication Data

Clairday, Robynn.
    Postcards from World War II : sights & sentiments from the last
century / Robynn Clairday, Matt Clairday.
       p. cm.
    ISBN 0-7570-0102-5 (quality pbk.)
    1. World War, 1939–1945—United States.   2. Postcards—United States.
I. Title: Postcards from World War Two.   II. Title: Postcards from World
War 2.   III. Clairday, Matt.   IV. Title.
    D769 .C53 2002
    940.53'73—dc21

2001004139

Printed in the United States of America

10   9   8   7   6   5   4   3   2   1

Contents

Johnie Washington Clairday

Sanford Jerome Reisler

We dedicate this book
to our fathers,
Johnie Washington Clairday
and
Sanford Jerome Reisler,
who served in the war.

Introduction

War meant separation. American girls kissed their men goodbye and pledged not to "sit under the apple tree" with anyone but their true love.

It is 1942. As war rages throughout the world, a young American G.I. has just received final orders—in less than an hour he will be shipping out to an unspecified destination in northern Africa. With only a few free minutes to send a message back home, he grabs a postcard and scribbles a note to his bride. He tells her that he is doing well. He has just gotten his marching orders, so it may be some time before he can write to her again. He sends his love, asks her to write, and then adds one last thought—tonight she'll be in his dreams. A number of days later, his young wife receives the message with tears and gratitude. For that fleeting, fragile moment, the few words on this small card connect her to her husband so many miles away.

It is 1944. A wheat farmer, his chores done and the sun beginning to set, takes a slow walk to his roadside mailbox. He reaches inside. Amid a small handful of mail, he spots it—a colorful postcard from his son who is stationed somewhere in the Pacific. He flips the postcard over and spies his son's familiar scrawl. He smiles. The message is brief, but warm and reassuring, and for that instant, although thousands of miles from home, that son has reached out and hugged his dad.

During World War II, postcards, both private and government issue, created important links, connecting tens of thousands of servicemen to their friends and family back home. It was the soldier's quickest and most convenient means of communicating thoughts and feelings to distant loved ones. No matter what the message may have said, every postcard was a way of saying, "I'm okay" and "I'm thinking of you." In a world of doubt and devastation, it was an affirmation of life.

War World II was the worst war in all history—a conflict in which the forces for democracy and freedom battled the rising tide of fascism and tyranny. It was a time of ferocious battles waged on land, sea, and in the air; when the entire planet seemed to tremble with the fear of annihilation; when millions faced a daily struggle for survival. Determined to stop the Axis powers from seizing world domination, the Allies had vowed to do whatever was necessary to defeat them. And the uncertainty was enormous. No one could say what the outcome would be—at what personal cost the future would be secured.

Postcards from World War II is not a historical account of this turbulent period, but offers poignant, everyday views of servicemen and women caught up in the war. The words penned on the backs of these small cards were actually written by those who lived—and perhaps died—during this fight for freedom. Although brief, these communications convey a sense of the emotions—the fear and courage, the love and humor, the anguish and pride—that characterized the people serving their country so far from home.

War is always a big story. Amid the facts and figures of victories won and battles lost, it is easy to forget that the combatants were individuals with their own lives and personal stories. The postcards in this book present their distinctive tales. You'll read the words of a young recruit who has written a few lines to his mother from boot camp. It is the farthest he has ever been from home, and his words convey how lonely and homesick he is. Although he is scared, he wants to be brave; but he's overwhelmed with the desire to sleep in his own bed . . .

A melancholy soldier sends heartfelt words of love and tenderness to his children at Christmas. He reminds them how much their Daddy loves and misses them, and how he longs to be with them during the holiday season . . .

The humor of the fighting men is apparent on this Pacific island signpost.

Connection with home—by letter, postcard, or V-mail—
was vital to the morale of America's fighting men.

A sailor who has just been notified of an up-and-coming leave writes excitedly to his girl back home. He tells her to start making wedding plans . . .

During World War II, the postcard was a near-perfect way to keep in touch. Soldiers didn't always have the time to write letters. In boot camp, they were often too exhausted to write more than a paragraph. Life was terribly uncertain and fragile, not just for those fighting for freedom and democracy, but also for those who remained at home. The postcard enabled the soldier to quickly tell his wife or mother or neighbor or child that he was alive and thinking of them. It allowed him to reach out and make a connection.

Postcards from WWII provides us with brief glimpses into the lives of those who served their country during this uncertain, terrifying period. Their written words enable us to peek into their souls. Beginning with 1941, each chapter represents a year of the war and includes postcards that were sent during that same year. The authors of the postcards came from all over the United States—from both coasts, the Midwest, the Plains, and the South. They trained in camps from California to North Carolina and from Michigan to Texas. They flew fighter planes and drove tanks. They learned how to use arms and march and fight and survive. They fought in every part of the world, but they longed for the comfort and familiarity of home.

If the eyes are the windows to the soul, letters reflect the workings of the heart. In 1943, the average American soldier received fourteen pieces of mail a week, but most of these cards and letters have been lost. Much of their return mail, however, like the postcards in this book, still exists. These cards reveal the humor, the raw loneliness, the simple honesty, and the hearts of the men and women who sent them. Each postcard is truly a part of our collective American history, a tangible memory of the heroism of the "greatest" generation.

"We are now in this war. We are all in it all the way.
Every single man, woman, and child is a partner
in the most tremendous undertaking of our American history.
We must share together the bad news and the good news,
the defeats and the victories, the changing fortunes of war. . . .
And in the dark hours of this day and through
dark days that may yet to come, we will know that the vast
majority of the members of the human race are on
our side. Many of them are fighting with us. All of them are
praying for us. For, in representing our cause, we represent
theirs, as well our hope and their hope for liberty under God."

President Franklin Delano Roosevelt
Radio Address, December 9, 1941

1941

In the fall of 1941, the war in Europe was already two years old. France had fallen, England stood alone, and the relentless German blitzkrieg was advancing through southern Russia. Across the Atlantic, the United States was being drawn ever closer to direct involvement in the war as it provided aid to beleaguered Europeans. In Asia, the armed forces of Japan were moving toward full domination of China, Southeast Asia, and the Southwest Pacific. The Axis powers were an unstoppable triad, and the United States seemed certain to be a target of their aggression. In 1941, America prepared for war.

While maintaining a neutral position, President Franklin D. Roosevelt had begun the buildup of the country's armed forces in 1939. Only the American Navy was a strong fighting force, and an immediate appropriation of $575 million had been made for Air Corps expansion. But the Army was, in the words of General George Marshall, a "midget force" of only 137,000 men; it was smaller in size than the army of Portugal. After Germany invaded Poland in 1939, Roosevelt had declared a limited national emergency, and the country's regular Army was increased to 227,000 against the advice of many members of Congress. As the war consumed Europe, Amer-

icans gradually became aware that the nation had to prepare itself for possible conflict. In 1940, when the President asked Congress for 50,000 new aircraft, there was little opposition, and by the end of July, a once-reluctant Congress had appropriated $12 billion for defense. On September 16, Roosevelt signed the Selective Service and Training Act—a bill that authorized the registration of all men aged twenty-one to thirty-five, and the drafting of 900,000.

As the Germans wrested control of Europe, America took another dramatic step "to promote the defense" of the country without sacrificing its neutrality. The Lend-Lease Act in March of 1941 gave President Roosevelt power to sell, transfer, lend, or lease aircraft and other military aid to the Allies. By the end of 1941, the arming of merchant shipping had brought the United States into a violent but "undeclared" war against Germany.

The drift toward war was also apparent in Washington's economic support of the Allies. The Roosevelt Administration imposed domestic price controls and froze German and Italian assets in its forlorn effort to fight the Axis powers through non-military means. Fearing that Japan was a threat to the U.S.-controlled Philippines, Roosevelt froze Japanese assets that were held in the United States.

Embargoes against oil and steel exports soon followed. Then on December 7, 1941, the Japanese launched a surprise air attack, which devastated the U.S. naval base at Pearl Harbor in Hawaii and killed about 3,000 Americans. An outraged Roosevelt condemned the day of "infamy," and immediately asked Congress to declare war against the Empire of Japan. Three days later, when Germany declared war on the U.S., the war in Europe became a world war.

Although war had been approaching for two years, few Americans anticipated such an immediate and dramatic entry. Stunned and reeling from the Pearl Harbor attack, the nation—once divided in its feelings on entering the war—came together in a surge of patriotic loyalty to present a united front against the Axis powers. Fueled by outrage, the mood during those last weeks of 1941 was one of determination and anger. That common attitude—within the military and on the domestic front—kept the country unified over the course of the next few years. The nation was about to experience dramatic changes that would shape its future and profoundly affect its people. Many of these changes, however, were already in place.

In May of 1941, President Roosevelt purchased the first Series E United States Savings Bond from Secretary of the Treasury Henry Morgenthau. Once the country entered the war, these war bonds would fast become a symbol of patriotism. The draft had been renewed and as the services recruited men, there was an unexpected push for women to serve in the military. Congresswoman Edith Nourse Rogers introduced the WAAC (Women's Army Auxiliary Corps) bill to Congress in 1941. Over 150,000 women served in the Corps during the war, receiving both status and benefits. In addition, the years 1941 to 1945 forever changed the role of women on the domestic front. Once fighting began, many jobs previously held by men became the responsibility of women.

During this last year of peace, Americans enjoyed a cultural bonanza. Big band music, jazz, and swing filled the air. Glenn Miller's spirited "Chattanooga Choo-Choo" was released, as was his immortal rendition of "Blueberry Hill." The Andrews Sisters came out with "Bounce Me Brother with a Solid Four," and the world's most popular vocalist, Bing Crosby, recorded songs like "I Ain't Got Nobody" and "You Are My Sunshine." The famous children's book *Curious George* by H.A. Rey was published in 1941, and *Call It Courage* by Armstrong Sperry was the Newbery Award winner. The classic films *Citizen Kane* and *The Maltese Falcon* were also released that year. The popular crime fighter called *The Shadow* drew listeners to the radio, while a new form of entertainment called *soundies* was developed in January of 1941. These short black-and-white 16-millimeter films were shown on coin-operated projection machines called *panorams*, which were found in nightclubs, bars, and restaurants. Soundies often featured a variety of song and dance performances that were spliced together on a reel that ran in a continuous loop.

Such cheery entertainment became less frequent during the ensuing years. Americans harshly discovered that the world was a dangerous place. No one knew what tomorrow would bring.

3" Anti-Aircraft Battery, Fort Sheridan, Illinois

OB-H2528

Hello "Speed" I arrived here all
in decent shape and progressing thru
the course quiet steady. Not no
practical work but intend to start
the next wk sometime. Tell Charles
and Squeak to write besides yourself
when answering. Would have write sooner
but been studying hard an etc are
you still going to B.C. and Albion
rolling skating. as yet, and getting
charless horses Ha! Ha! Us fellows
from Custer here for this school all
say hello and write. Save this
card for me will you because
I want to give it to Esther my girl
friend. Your old room pal.
Allan K. Pritchard Jr.
Quarter master Corp, Det. Fort Sheridan, Ill.

POST CARD

Wilbur "Speed" Jordan
Quarter master, Corp. Post.
Fort Custer, Michigan

PHOTOS BY U. S. ARMY SIGNAL CORPS   U. S. Field Artillery   © CURT TEICH & CO., INC.

Camp Grant, Ill.
aug. 27, 1941

Dear Mother & Dad.

Here I am in the U. S. Army., & so far its not too bad. Don't know how long I'll be here — probably just a few days & then again it might be a few months. They don't tell you very much here, so you have to find out for yourself or not at all.

Food here is very good for Army life — we do have beans, but also other things. Had Watermelon for lunch.

Been busy all day & am going to shave & go to bed. Will write later. Let Grandma & the rest know where I am for now. Don't send anything here for awhile, outside of a letter or so because I may be moved, & may not get it.

address: Co. "B"
Barracks 215
Camp Grant, Ill.

Love, Sam,
Edwin

AIR VIEW LOOKING NORTH, CAMP GRANT, ILL.

©R.P.S.

POSTCARD

★★★★★★★★★★★★★★★★★★★★★★★★★★★★★★★★★★★★★★★

Correspondence   Address

Hello Jigs,
    Well they got me
in the army now, and
its not bad. They are
going to make a pil pusher
out of me. Im in the 26th
Battalion of a medical
training Center Co A.
Bldg. 308. Camp Grant, Ill.
It took me a long time to
write but I thought that
you might want to know
where I am   your Pal George

MR. VINCENT Schement
36 DAYTON DR.
OSBORN, OHIO

10-22-41

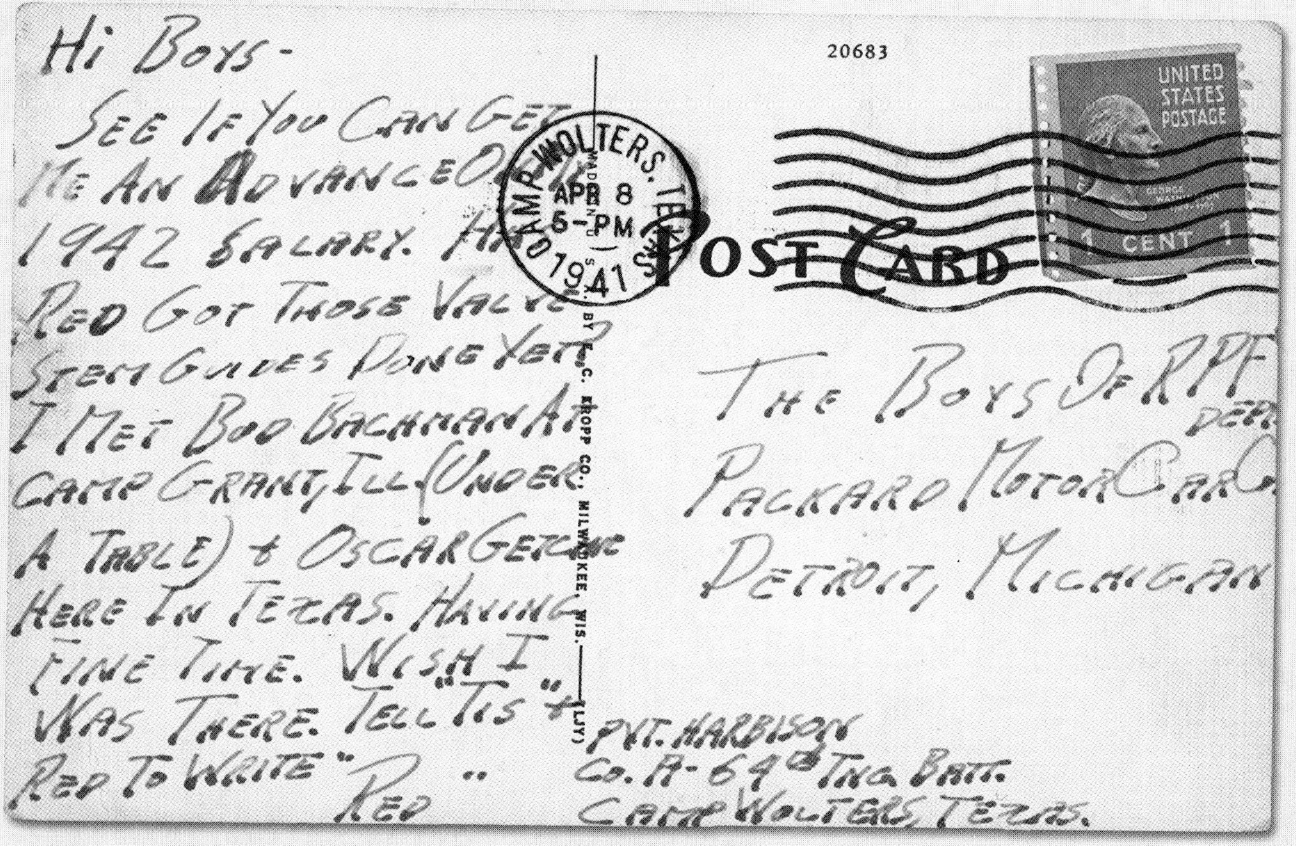

Hi Boys—
See If You Can Get
Me An Advance On
1942 Salary. Has
Red Got Those Valve
Stem Guides Done Yet?
I Met Bob Bachman At
Camp Grant, Ill. (Under
A Table) & Oscar Geller
Here In Texas. Having
Fine Time. Wish I
Was There. Tell "Tis" &
Red To Write"
                Red

20683

CAMP WOLTERS, TEXAS
APR 8
5-PM
1941

POST CARD

UNITED STATES
POSTAGE
GEORGE WASHINGTON
1 CENT 1

The Boys Of R.P.F.
                        Dept.
Packard Motor Car Co.
Detroit, Michigan

Pvt. Harbison
Co. A-64th Tng. Batt.
Camp Wolters, Texas.

You're in the Service Now

In September 1939, as the German blitzkrieg enveloped Poland and Europe went to war, the career Army of the United States totaled 137,000 men. Over the next year, advocates of American "preparedness" contended with Congressional isolationists in an extended battle over drafting young men into military service. Because 1940 was an election year, President Franklin D. Roosevelt delayed endorsing selective service until his acceptance speech for a third nomination, but he provided the final impetus for passage of the Burke-Wadsworth Act—more commonly known as the Selective Service Act—on September 16, 1940. Under this bill, men aged eighteen to thirty-five were liable for a year of military service, and the President signed it despite candlelight vigils held in protest outside the White House.

The fight over the draft continued even as Hitler conquered Europe. America First supporters vehemently opposed any extension of the draft, and it was by the margin of a single vote in the House that the term of enlistment was extended by eighteen months in August of 1941. Moreover, the draft age was expanded to include those from age eighteen to forty-three. After Pearl Harbor, however, the nation came together and rallied behind its President, steeling itself for the battles and suffering ahead.

Many questioned if the United States had the ability to create a modern Army in time to defeat the Axis powers. Of the nearly 20 million people affected by the Selective Service System, over 10 million were inducted; 5 million volunteers were accepted, including 330,000 women. The majority of draftees were inducted into the Army, and they proudly accepted the call to serve.

Once a man's number came up and he received "greetings" from the draft board, he reported to an induction station where he underwent a thorough physical exam. Fully 40 percent

"This Is the Army, Mr. Jones." America may have been unprepared for total war, but every soldier learned to dig.

You're in the Service Now

of the first million draftees were found unfit to serve due to nutritional or dental problems. Those who passed were sent home for two weeks to settle their affairs. When they reported back, they belonged to the Army. They received haircuts, inoculations, and fatigue olive drabs, and then went off to the "boot camp" experience, which most would remember forever as the hardest days of their lives. On average, these soldiers were about one inch taller and eight pounds heavier than the "doughboys" of WWI, but they would prove to have the same ability to act independently.

The average soldier had two years of high school, knew no foreign language, and had never fired a gun. He was part of a military force that was created "without traditions and useless theories," an army of civilians that won the praise of Field Marshal Erwin Rommel. The American soldier was part of an army that never lost its desire to "go home," but that understood it had a job to do first. In 1945, with a total of 8.3 million men under arms, the U.S. Army had become the world's most elite fighting force. It could never have been accomplished without the Selective Service System.

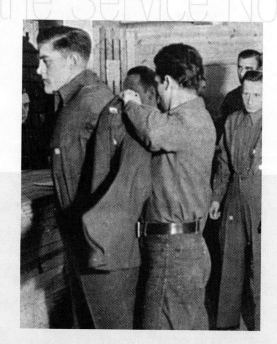

During the first year of the draft, there was a uniform shortage, and many new soldiers received second-hand clothing.

Tanks Ready for Maneuvers

M3

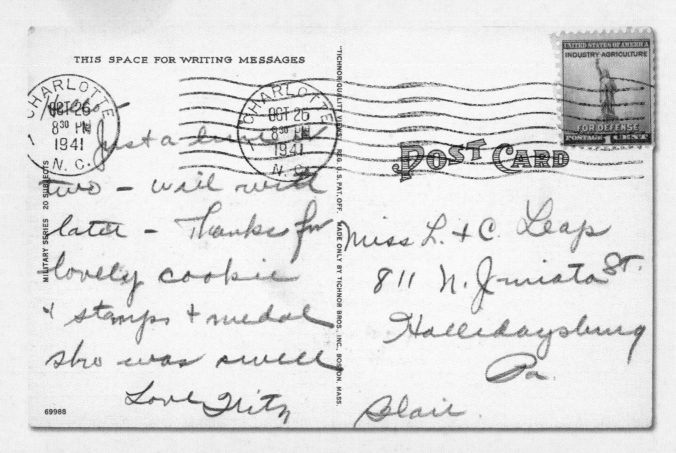

THIS SPACE FOR WRITING MESSAGES

CHARLOTTE
OCT 26
8³⁰ PM
1941
N.C.

CHARLOTTE
OCT 26
8³⁰ PM
1941
N.C.

POST CARD

Just a line or
two — will write
later — Thanks for
lovely cookie
& stamps & medal
she was swell
Love Fitz

MILITARY SERIES 20 SUBJECTS

"TICHNOR QUALITY VIEWS," REG. U.S. PAT. OFF. MADE ONLY BY TICHNOR BROS. INC., BOSTON, MASS.

Miss L. & C. Leap
811 N. Juniata St.
Hollidaysburg
Pa.
Blair.

69988

UNITED STATES OF AMERICA
INDUSTRY AGRICULTURE
FOR DEFENSE
POSTAGE 1 CENT

No. 304   INFANTRY ADVANCE, SUPPORTED BY TANKS THROUGH SMOKE SCREEN

Troy – 13/1/41

Hi Ed. Been working like
a beaver the last two
days. Was taken from
duty this afternoon
& filled out a bunch
of papers. Seen
discharg. papers,
my Service Regist. discharge,
distinguished them, is
Dec – About Christmas, will
see. Hope see it Sunday.

Defend Your Country—
Join the U. S. Army.

THIS SPACE FOR MESSAGE

POST CARD

THIS SPACE FOR ADDRESS ONLY

UNITED STATES POSTAGE
1 CENT

W. R. THOMPSON & COMPANY, PUBLISHERS, RICHMOND, VIRGINIA

Edward McPhartlin,

Hastings,

Michigan.

R. F. D. 1.

On January 1, 1942, the United States, Great Britain, and twenty-four other Allies signed the United Nations Declaration. Those signing this document pledged mutual assistance to one another and promised not to enter into individual peace agreements with the Axis powers. This was the first official use of the term "United Nations." Optimists believed it promised a better world in the future.

For the most part, 1942 was a year of disasters with only hints of victory. After Pearl Harbor, the Japanese won a series of victories in Bataan, Corregidor, and Singapore. Japan appeared to be undefeatable until the Battle of Midway on June 4, a naval victory that marked a turning point in the Pacific war. The Japanese First Air Fleet lost four carriers and suffered significant casualties for the first time, as the United States successfully blunted their steady advance. In August, U.S. forces landed at Guadalcanal, and began a seven-month fight to retake the island from the Japanese.

In the European theater, the entry of the United States gave renewed hope to Britain and Russia. The fight for air dominance was savage as Germany continued bombing Britain, but now a strength-ened Royal Air Force (RAF) retaliated with air raids of its own, assaulting the German city of Cologne in May. In August, America's "flying fortresses" launched their first independent attack in Europe, as the Eighth Air Force destroyed railroad yards in Rouen. But these were minor affairs compared with the titanic battle being waged in southern Russia for control of the city of Stalingrad. German and Russian armies were locked in a death grip, which neither could afford to lose. As that battle continued, British General Bernard Montgomery won a clear victory in the African desert over Rommel's German-Italian army. The victory at El Alamein eliminated the German threat to the Suez Canal and the Middle East. During this time, U.S. forces made their presence known as they landed near Casablanca in North Africa.

For the United States, 1942 was a year spent primarily in preparation for war in Europe. In March, the Army was split into three divisions—Air Forces, Ground Forces, and Service Forces—but all suffered from shortages of equipment and trained personnel.

The demands of the conflict became evident in American home life as civilians started to realize more fully the sacrifices they were expected to make. In April, President Roosevelt described his home front expectations: "One front and one battle where everyone in the United States—every man, woman, and child—is in action. That front is right here at home, in our daily lives." Everyone had a personal stake in the war.

Gradually, the nation was converted to a full wartime effort. Existing auto plants began manufacturing jeeps, tanks, and other equipment, while tremendous new facilities were constructed throughout the country for the production of military goods. The United States would produce 296,000 planes, 107,000 tanks, 71,000 ships, and 20 million rifles by 1945. To intensify the effort, energy-saving Daylight Saving Time went into effect in February.

Soon, everyone began to experience the rigors of total war. The government set controls on pricing, wages, supplies, and essential spending, while its Office of Price Administration (OPA) issued the first war ration books. Goods like sugar, gasoline, butter, and cheese became scarce, while certain raw materials that were needed for the war effort were funneled toward the military. Nylon in particular became precious, and women drew lines on the backs of their bare legs with eyebrow pencil to simulate seamed stockings. They also began wearing shorter skirts to save on material. Travel became difficult due to the rationing of gasoline. For recreation, people turned to inexpensive means of amusement, which meant participating in life's more simple pleasures. "Going out" often meant getting together with family or neighbors at someone's home.

Americans were united behind their servicemen and supported the war, but they still found time to play. Board games like chess and checkers were popular, and listening to the radio was a typical means of getting news and enjoying music and radio shows. Movies provided a welcome escape from the stresses of wartime life, and no period of our history had greater theater attendance. People flocked to theaters where they watched Humphrey Bogart and Ingrid Bergman heat up the screen in *Casablanca*, while movies like Abbott and Costello's *Rio Rita* and *Who Done It?* provided much-needed comic relief. Young readers perused the first *Little Golden Books*, which were destined to become classics. Everyone enjoyed the story of *The Secret Life of Walter Mitty*, while more serious readers turned to Albert Camus' novel *The Stranger*.

Popular music featured Bing Crosby's "White Christmas," Kate Smith's "He Wears a Pair of Silver Wings," and the Andrews Sisters' "Don't Sit Under the Apple Tree." Frank Sinatra, the bobby-soxers' heartthrob, sang with the Tommy Dorsey Orchestra, and on December 31, 1942, made his solo debut in New York City. Dizzy Gillespie gained attention as part of the bebop movement in Harlem.

The year 1942 was a time of transition as the nation came to understand the costs of world war. Citizens found themselves facing an uncertain world, and if the great battles were yet to be fought, the increasing casualty lists indicated that the cost of victory would be very great. As the military geared up for battle, the country built up its courageous spirit for the trials ahead.

AC4:—READY TO TAKE OFF ON A NIGHT TRAINING FLIGHT.

Photo by Acme

LANGLEY FIELD, VA.

48196

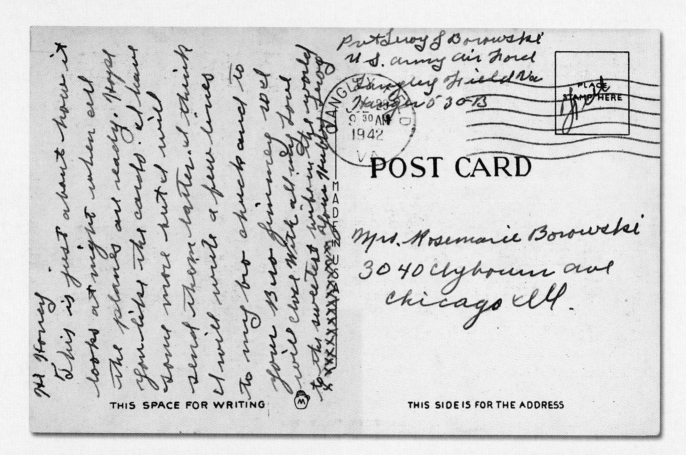

THIS SPACE FOR WRITING

THIS SIDE IS FOR THE ADDRESS

MADE IN U.S.A.

Pvt Leroy J Borowski
U.S. Army Air Force
Langley Field Va
Hangar 5 30 B

POST CARD

Mrs. Rosemarie Borowski
3040 Clybourn Ave
Chicago Ill.

USA-33

Machine Gun Training

PHOTO BY U.S. ARMY SIGNAL CORPS

1B-H184

Pvt. C.L. Tennent Jr.
A.P.O. 912 % P.M.
N.Y. - N.Y.

BROOKLYN N.Y. JAN 17 PM 42

BUY DEFENSE SAVINGS BONDS AND STAMPS

UNITED STATES OF AMERICA
INDUSTRY·AGRICULTURE
FOR DEFENSE
POSTAGE CENT

POST CARD

U.S. ARMY SERIES

GENUINE CURTEICH-CHICAGO "C.T. ART-COLORTONE" POST CARD (REG. U.S. PAT. OFF.)

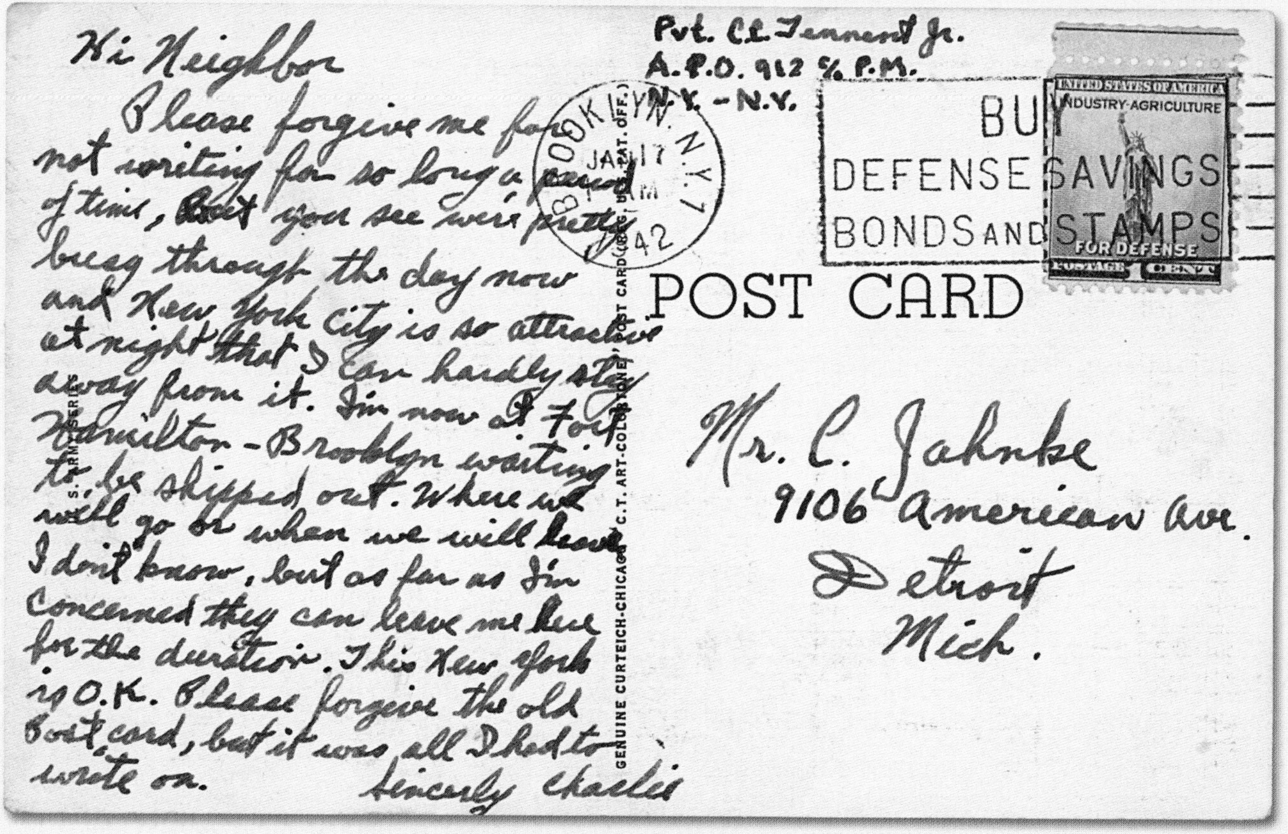

Hi Neighbor

Please forgive me for not writing for so long a period of time, but you see we're pretty busy through the day now and New York City is so attractive at night that I can hardly stay away from it. I'm now at Fort Hamilton - Brooklyn waiting to be shipped out. Where we will go or when we will leave I don't know, but as far as I'm concerned they can leave me here for the duration. This New York is O.K. Please forgive the old post card, but it was all I had to write on.

Sincerely Charles

Mr. C. Jahnke
9106 American Ave.
Detroit
Mich.

Service Club, Fort Leonard Wood, Missouri

1B-H975

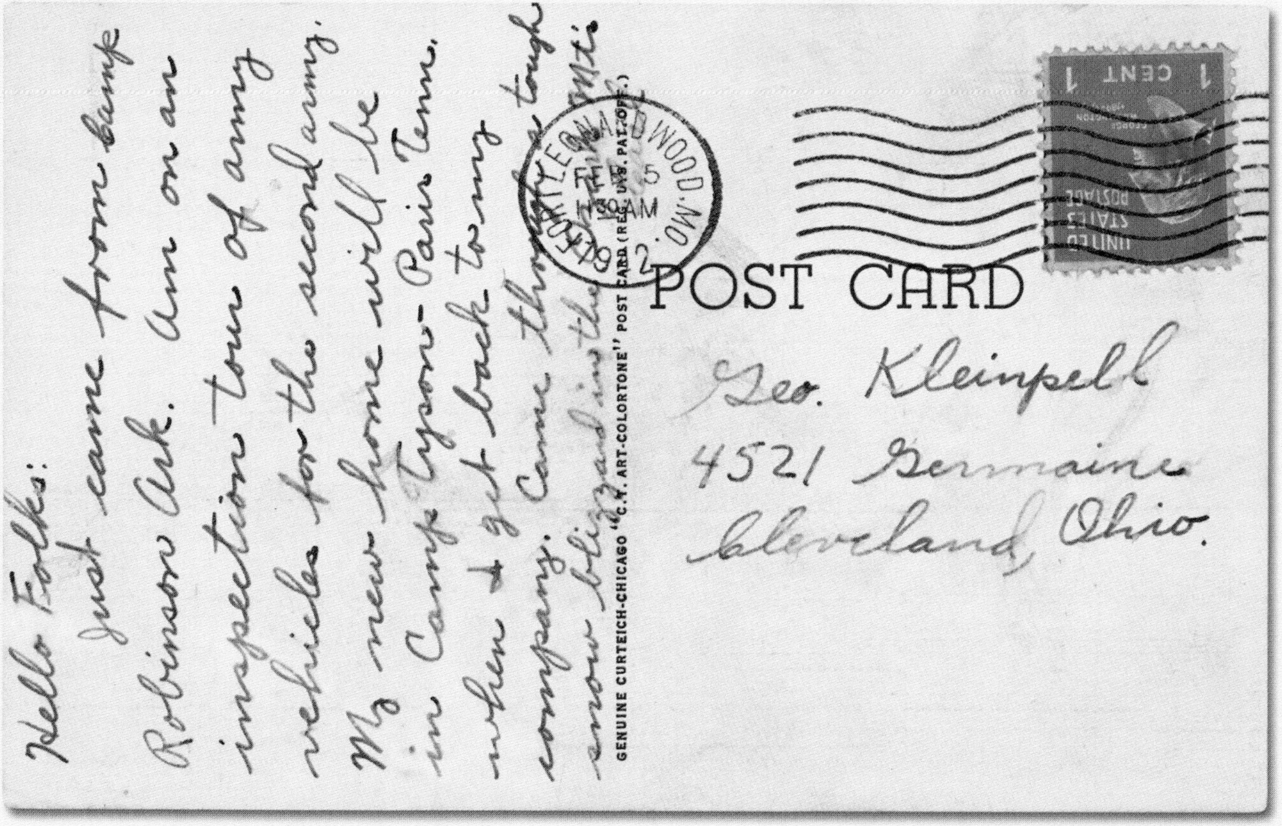

Hello Folks:
Just came from Camp Robinson Ark. Am on an inspection tour of army vehicles for the second army. My new home will be in Camp Tyson- Paris Tenn. when I get back to my company. Came through a tough snow blizzard in the ozarks.

GENUINE CURTEICH-CHICAGO "C.T. ART-COLORTONE" POST CARD (REG. U.S. PAT. OFF.)

FORT LEONARD WOOD, MO.
FEB 5 11:30 AM
1942

1 CENT 1
UNITED STATES POSTAGE

POST CARD

Geo. Kleinpell
4521 Germaine
Cleveland, Ohio.

Home Away from Home

Formed in 1941 in response to a request by President Franklin Roosevelt, the United Service Organization, more commonly known as the USO, was based on an idea conceived by General George C. Marshall. Its goal was to provide a "touch of home" for the country's rapidly growing members of the armed services when they were on leave. Through the joint efforts of six groups—the YMCA, YWCA, National Catholic Community Service, Jewish Welfare Board, Traveler's Aid Association, and Salvation Army— USO centers were established in over 3,000 communities during the war and run primarily by volunteers. Roosevelt was the organization's first Honorary Chairman—a position that has been held by every president since.

Centers were established quickly and in all sorts of unusual places. They sprung up in churches, barns, railroad cars, museums, castles, beach clubs, and log cabins, and they provided services that were as diverse as the locations themselves. Most centers offered recreational activities—dances were held; movies were shown; and, of course, the well-known free coffee and doughnuts were served. For some, USO bases provided a haven for spending a quiet moment alone or writing a letter home. Some centers offered spiritual guidance, and many made childcare available for military wives. A soldier could find almost anything he or she needed at the USO.

The organization became particularly famous for its live performances called *Camp Shows,* through which the entertainment industry helped boost the morale of its servicemen and women. During the war, these voluntary "soldiers in greasepaint" entertained the troops in military bases both at home and overseas, often placing their own lives in danger to do so. Many traveled through hazardous conditions to get to their destinations, and a few lost their lives

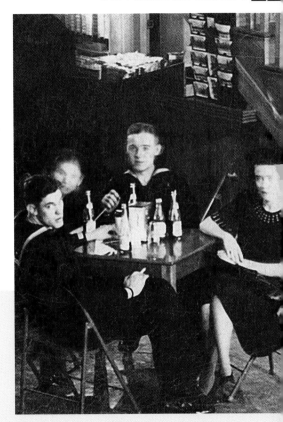

Churches, YMCAs, canteens, and the USO offered rest and relaxation to servicemen throughout the country.

when planes crashed or ships sank. Camp Show casts often performed on makeshift stages under extreme weather conditions, and it wasn't unusual for them to come under enemy fire.

In 1942, just a few months after the United States entered the war, comedian Bob Hope performed in his first overseas tour with the USO, kicking off a partnership with the organization that lasted over fifty years. Hope's variety shows included his signature monologs and comedic skits, a troupe of singers and dancers, and a beautiful woman or two. Hollywood, in general, was eager to show its patriotism, and lots of big names joined the ranks of USO entertainers. Screen siren Marlene Dietrich and popular pinup girl Betty Grable enthralled troops, while stars like Mickey Rooney, James Cagney, Bing Crosby, Gary Cooper, Clark Gable, and Laurel and Hardy offered their services as well. Other Camp Show celebs included Glenn Miller, Jack Benny, Humphrey Bogart, James Stewart, Fred Astaire, and the Andrews Sisters. Of course, not everyone who entertained with the USO shows was famous, but this didn't matter to the homesick soldiers, who were always enthusiastic and appreciative.

Between 1941 and 1947, with the help of over 7,000 entertainers, the USO put on nearly a half million performances. Its audiences were as small as twenty-five and as large as 15,000.

Involvement in the USO was one of the many ways in which the nation had come together to support the war effort. During this period, nearly 1.5 million Americans had volunteered their services in some way to the organization. After it was disbanded in 1947, the USO was revived in 1950 at the request of President Truman when the United States entered the Korean War. Still active today, the USO has nearly 120 locations worldwide, and continues to provide social, recreational, and spiritual facilities to members of the nation's armed services.

Tanks, U. S. Armored Division, Camp Chaffee, Ark.

1B-H185

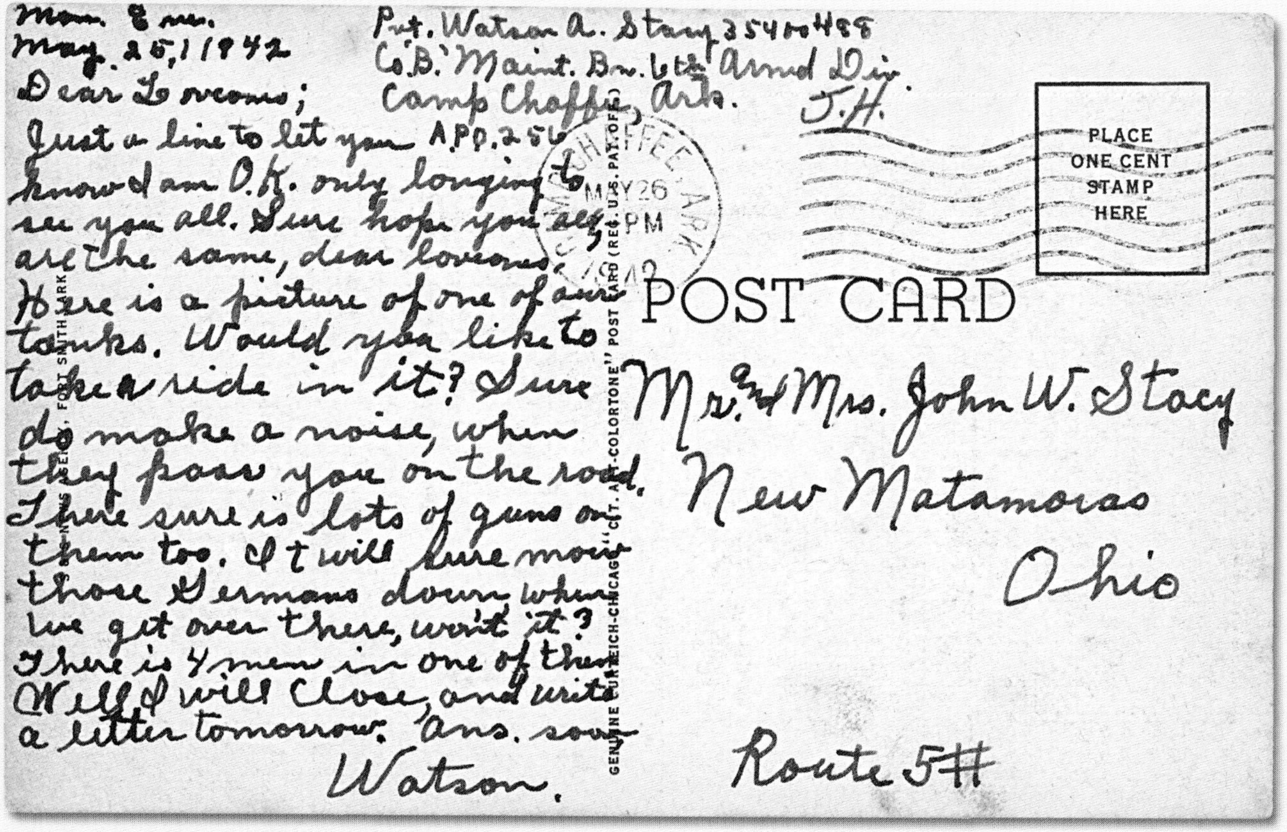

Mon. 8 am.
May 25, 1942

Pvt. Watson A. Stacy 35400488
Co. B. Maint. Bn. 6th Armd Div.
Camp Chaffee, Ark.
APO. 256

J.H.

Dear Loveones;
Just a line to let you know I am O.K. only longing to see you all. Sure hope you all are the same, dear loveones. Here is a picture of one of our tanks. Would you like to take a ride in it? Sure do make a noise, when they pass you on the road. There sure is lots of guns on them too. It will sure mow those Germans down when we get over there, won't it? There is 4 men in one of them. Well I will close, and write a letter tomorrow. Ans. soon
Watson.

CAMP CHAFFEE, ARK. MAY 26 PM 1942

PLACE ONE CENT STAMP HERE

POST CARD

GENUINE CURTEICH-CHICAGO "C.T. ART-COLORTONE" POST CARD (REG. U.S. PAT. OFF.)

FORT SMITH, ARK.

Mr. and Mrs. John W. Stacy
New Matamoras
Ohio
Route 5#

In 1942, American industry met the challenge of war and produced some 47,000 planes. Remember that "Rosie the Riveter" worked in an aircraft plant.

AIRPLANES BEING CONTROLLED BY RADIO—012

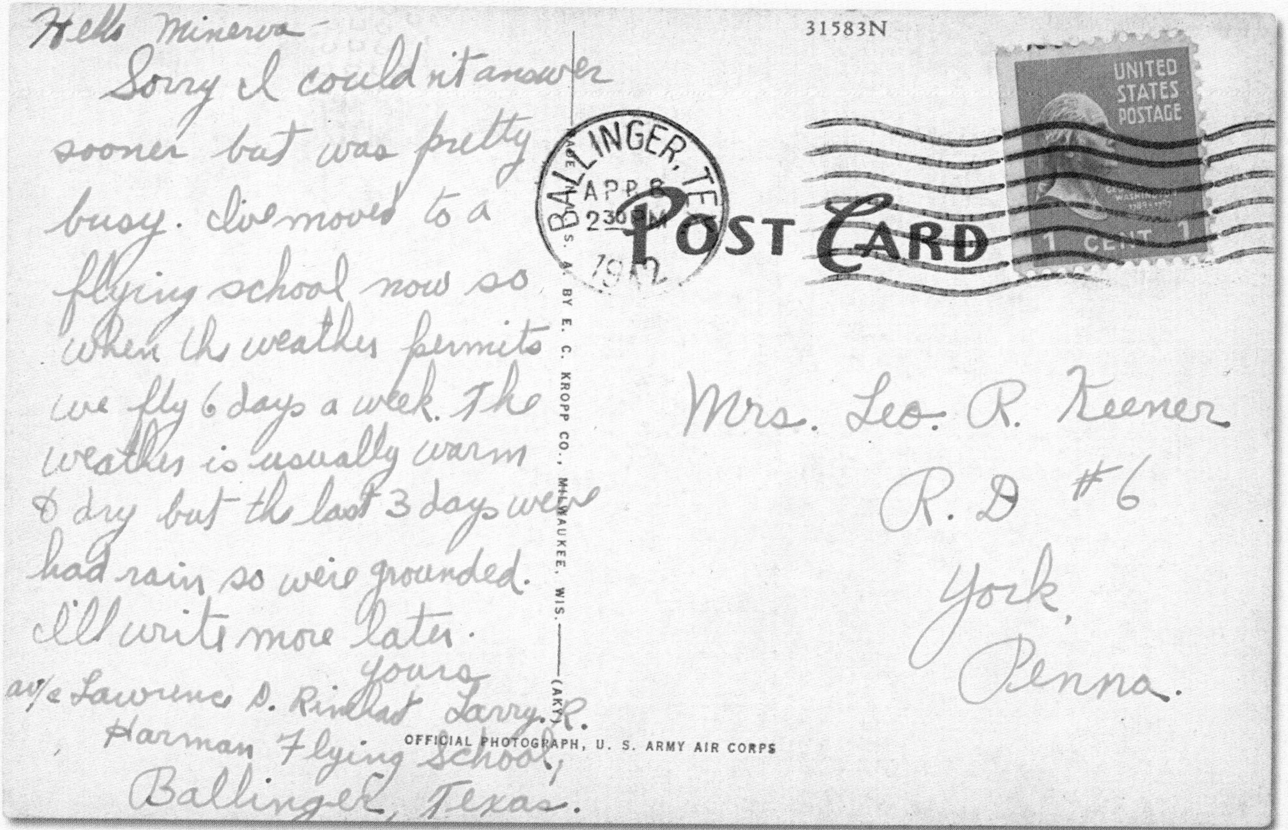

Hello Minerva -
Sorry I couldn't answer
sooner but was pretty
busy. I've moved to a
flying school now so
when the weather permits
we fly 6 days a week. The
weather is usually warm
& dry but the last 3 days we
had rain so were grounded.
I'll write more later.
Yours
A/c Lawrence D. Rineholt Larry. R.
Harman Flying school,
Ballinger, Texas.

31583N

BALLINGER, TEX.
APR 8
2 30 PM
1942

POST CARD

UNITED STATES POSTAGE
1 CENT 1

PUB. BY E. C. KROPP CO., MILWAUKEE, WIS. — (AK7)

OFFICIAL PHOTOGRAPH, U.S. ARMY AIR CORPS

Mrs. Leo. R. Keener
R. D #6
York,
Penna.

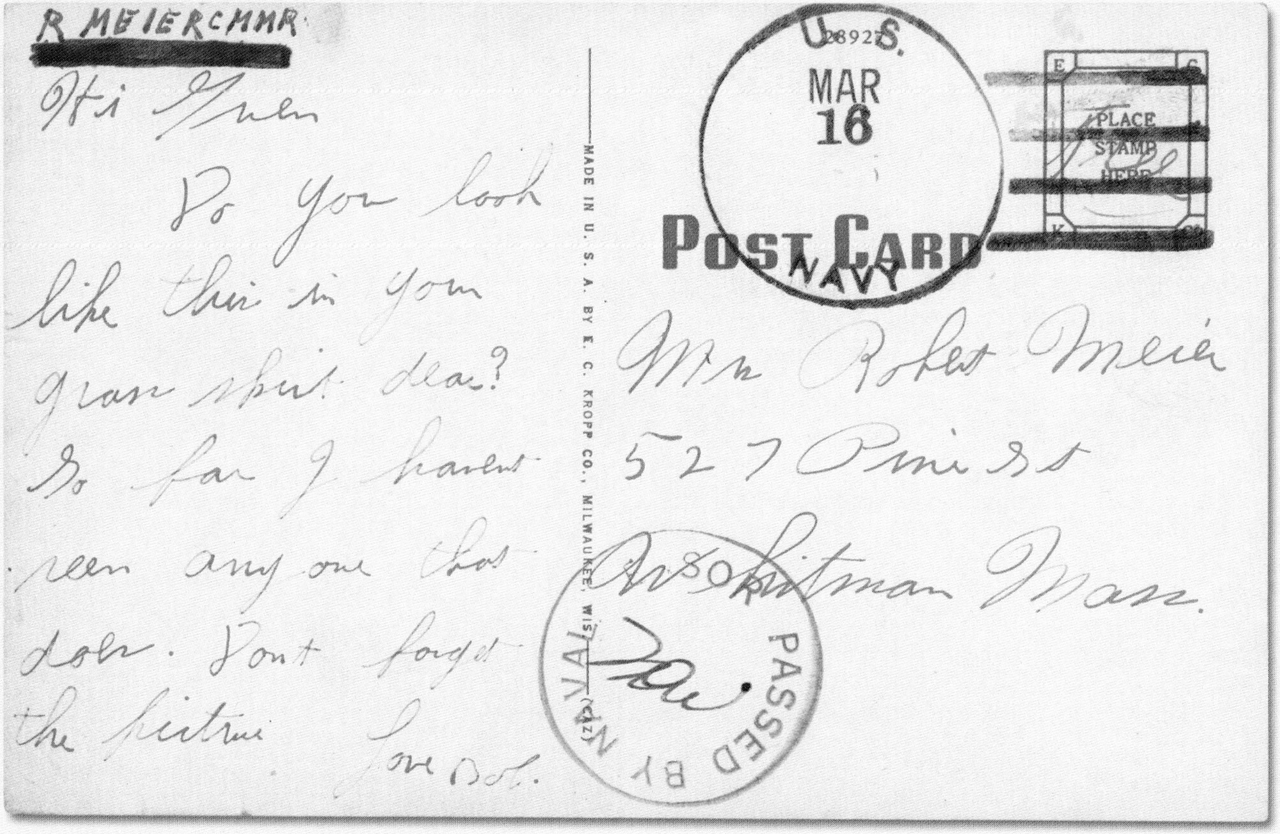

R MEIERCHNR

Hi Gwen

Do you look like this in your grass skirt dear? So far I haven't seen anyone that does. Don't forget the picture

Love Bob.

POST CARD

U.S.
MAR 16
NAVY

PASSED BY NAVAL

Mr Robert Meier
527 Pine St
Whitman Mass.

MADE IN U. S. A. BY E. C. KROPP CO., MILWAUKEE, WIS.

PLACE STAMP HERE

Checking Valves on Liquid Cooled Engine, Chanute Field, Rantoul, Ill.

PHOTO BY U. S. ARMY AIR CORPS

OB-H159S

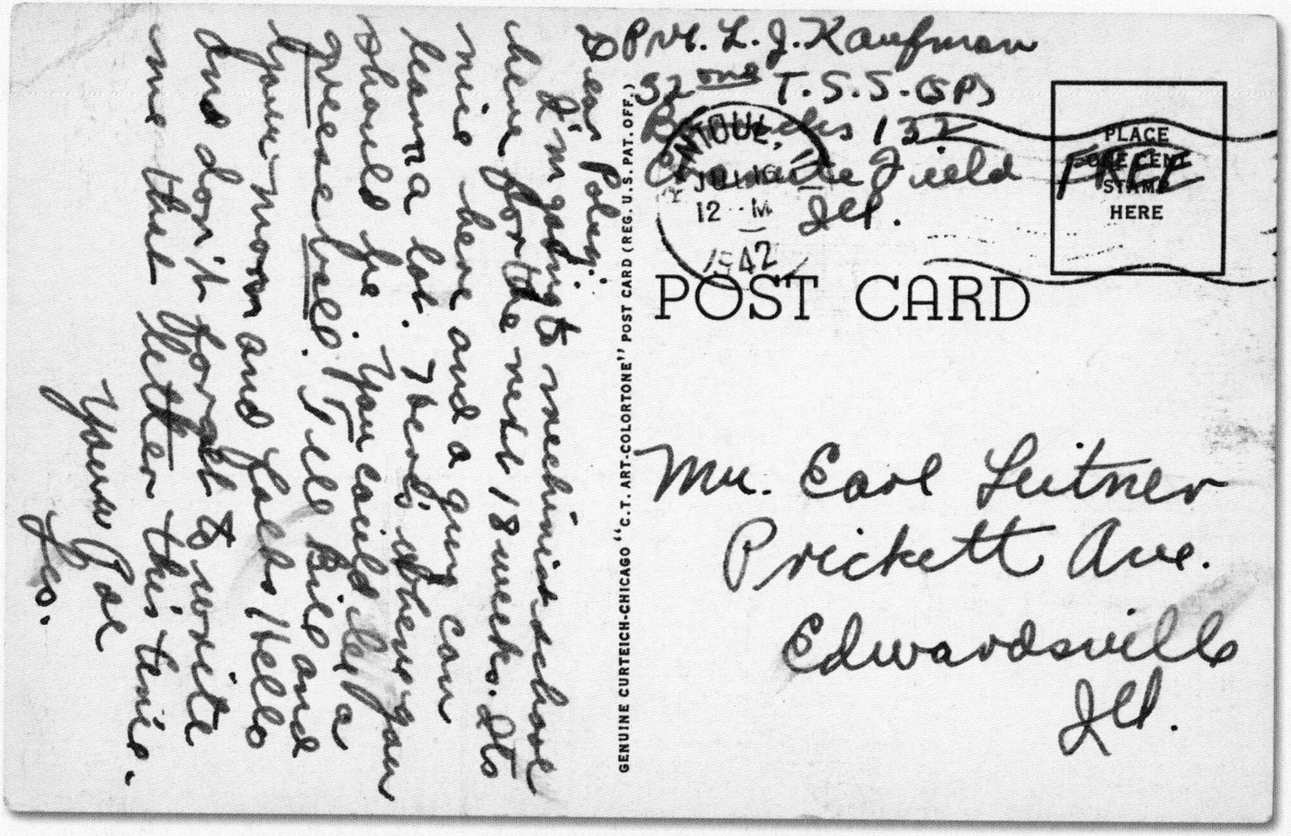

POST CARD

GENUINE CURTEICH-CHICAGO "C.T. ART-COLORTONE" POST CARD (REG. U.S. PAT. OFF.)

PLACE
ONE CENT
~~FREE~~
STAMP
HERE

Pvt. L. J. Kaufman
32nd T.S.S. (SP)
Chanute Field
Ill.

Dear Poley:

I'm getting a machine where
here for the next 18 weeks. It's
nice here and a guy can
learn a lot. Tell Henry I
should be there you
sure could tell a
machine tool. Tell Bill and
you mom and pals hello
and don't forget to write
me that letter this time.

Yours Pal
Leo.

Mr. Earl Leitner
Prickett Ave.
Edwardsville
Ill.

1159—Entrance to Fort Francis E. Warren, Cheyenne, Wyoming

Fort Francis E. Warren has been tremendously expanded since 1940 adding acres new barracks and thousands of soldiers. The new barracks are a training and replacement center for the Quartermaster Corps.

Private Charles F. Gorndt
Co M 2nd Rgt Qm Rtc
Ft F E Warren Wyo
Dear Son Glad to hear you
can drive the Car So good
take you feel good be nice
to Mother you will be well
And how is sandy Rabbits and
all the Chickens how is the Garden
I suppose you will be going to
School soon
From Daddy.

POST CARD

Robert. Gorndt
RFD #2 Brooklyn Station
Cleveland Ohio

1162--Replacement Center Barracks with Buildings of the Main Fort in Background, Fort Francis E. Warren, Cheyenne, Wyoming

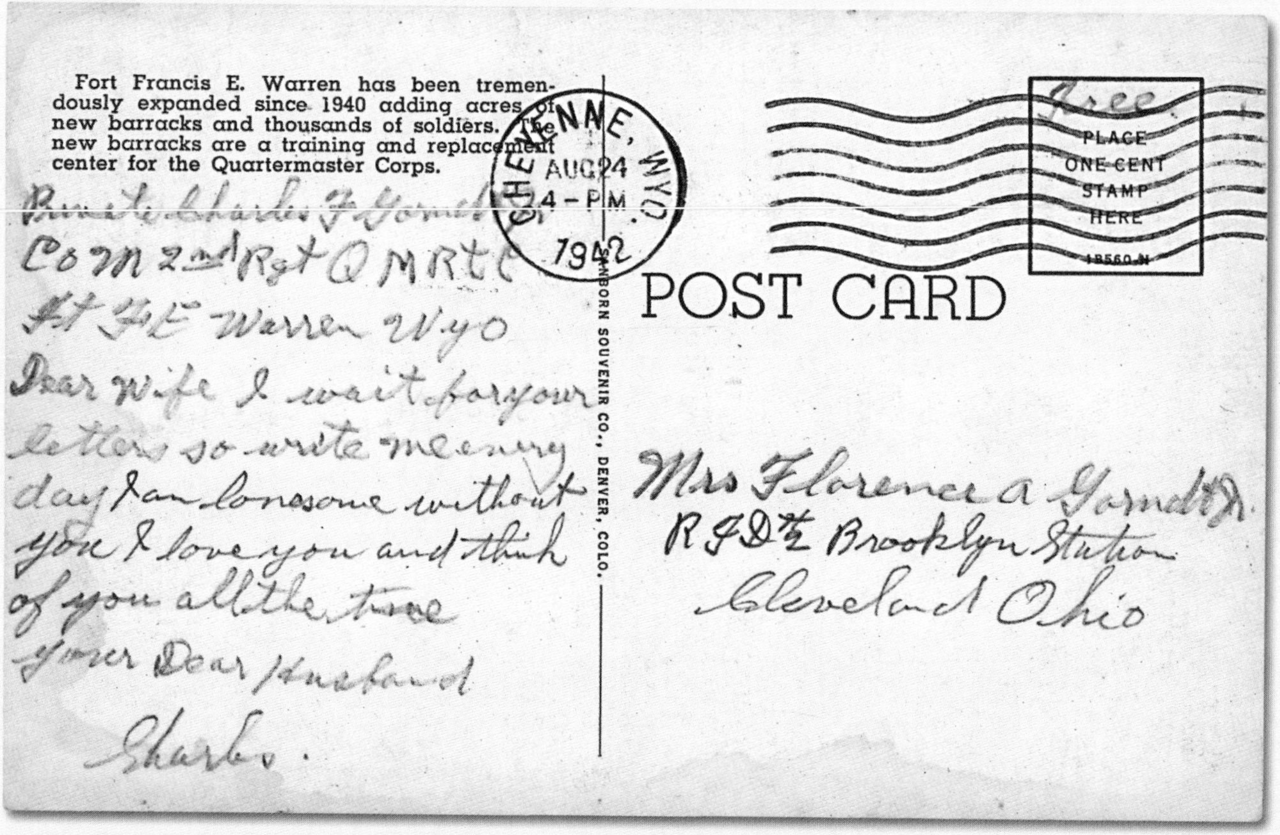

Fort Francis E. Warren has been tremendously expanded since 1940 adding acres of new barracks and thousands of soldiers. The new barracks are a training and replacement center for the Quartermaster Corps.

CHEYENNE, WYO.
AUG 24
4 — PM
1942

TAMBORN SOUVENIR CO., DENVER, COLO.

POST CARD

Free
PLACE
ONE CENT
STAMP
HERE
1B560 N

Private Charles F Garrett Sr
Co M 2nd Rgt Q M R T C
Ft F E Warren Wyo

Dear Wife I wait for your
letters so write me every
day I am lonesome without
you I love you and think
of you all the time
Your Dear Husband
Charles.

Mrs Florence a Garrett Sr
R J D ½ Brooklyn Station
Cleveland Ohio

No 312   37MM. ANTI-A RCRAFT GUN   Photo by U. S. Army Signal Corps.

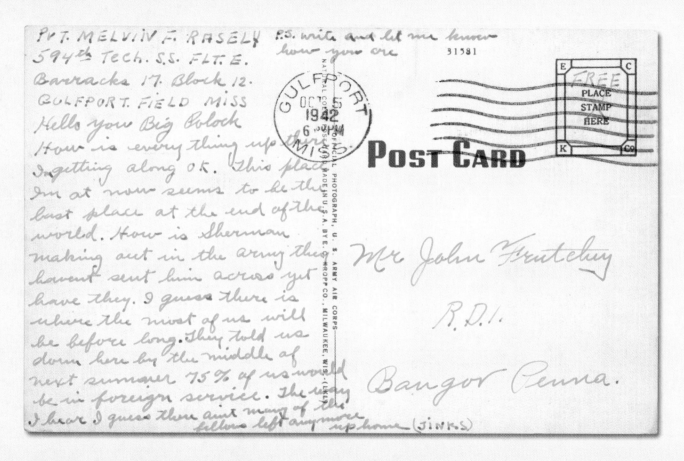

Pvt. MELVIN F. RASELY
594th Tech. S.S. FLT. E.
Barracks 17. Block 12.
GULFPORT. FIELD MISS

Hello you Big Polock
How is every thing up there
Im getting along ok. This place
Im at now seems to be the
last place at the end of the
world. How is Sherman
making out in the army they
havent sent him across yet
have they. I guess there is
where the most of us will
be before long. They told us
down here by the middle of
next summer 75% of us would
be in foreign service. The way
I hear I guess there aint many of the
fellows left anymore up home (JINKS)

P.S. write and let me know
how you are

31581

POST CARD

Mr John Frutchey
R.D. 1.
Bangor Penna.

Writing Home

Greetings From

Fort Custer

Mich.

Mess

Shining up

Playing Checkers

70479

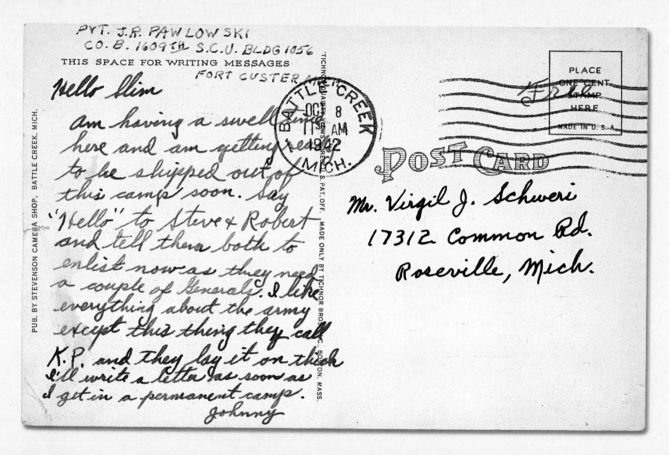

PVT. J.R. PAWLOWSKI
CO. B. 1609TH S.C.U. BLDG 1056
THIS SPACE FOR WRITING MESSAGES
FORT CUSTER MICH.

Hello Slim
    Am having a swell time
here and am getting ready
to be shipped out of
this camp soon. Say
"Hello" to Steve & Robert
and tell them both to
enlist now as they need
a couple of Generals. I like
everything about the army
except this thing they call
K.P. and they lay it on thick
I'll write a letter as soon as
I get in a permanent camp.
            Johnny

PUB. BY STEVENSON CAMERA SHOP, BATTLE CREEK, MICH.

"TICHNOGRAPH" (REG. U.S. PAT. OFF. MADE ONLY BY TICHNOR BROS. INC., BOSTON, MASS.

BATTLE CREEK
OCT 8
11 AM
1942
MICH.

POST CARD

PLACE
ONE CENT
STAMP
HERE
MADE IN U.S.A.

Mr. Virgil J. Schweri
17312 Common Rd.
Roseville, Mich.

WE BUILD AND FIGHT WITH ALL OUR MIGHT!

SEABEES

UNITED STATES NAVAL CONSTRUCTION BATTALIONS

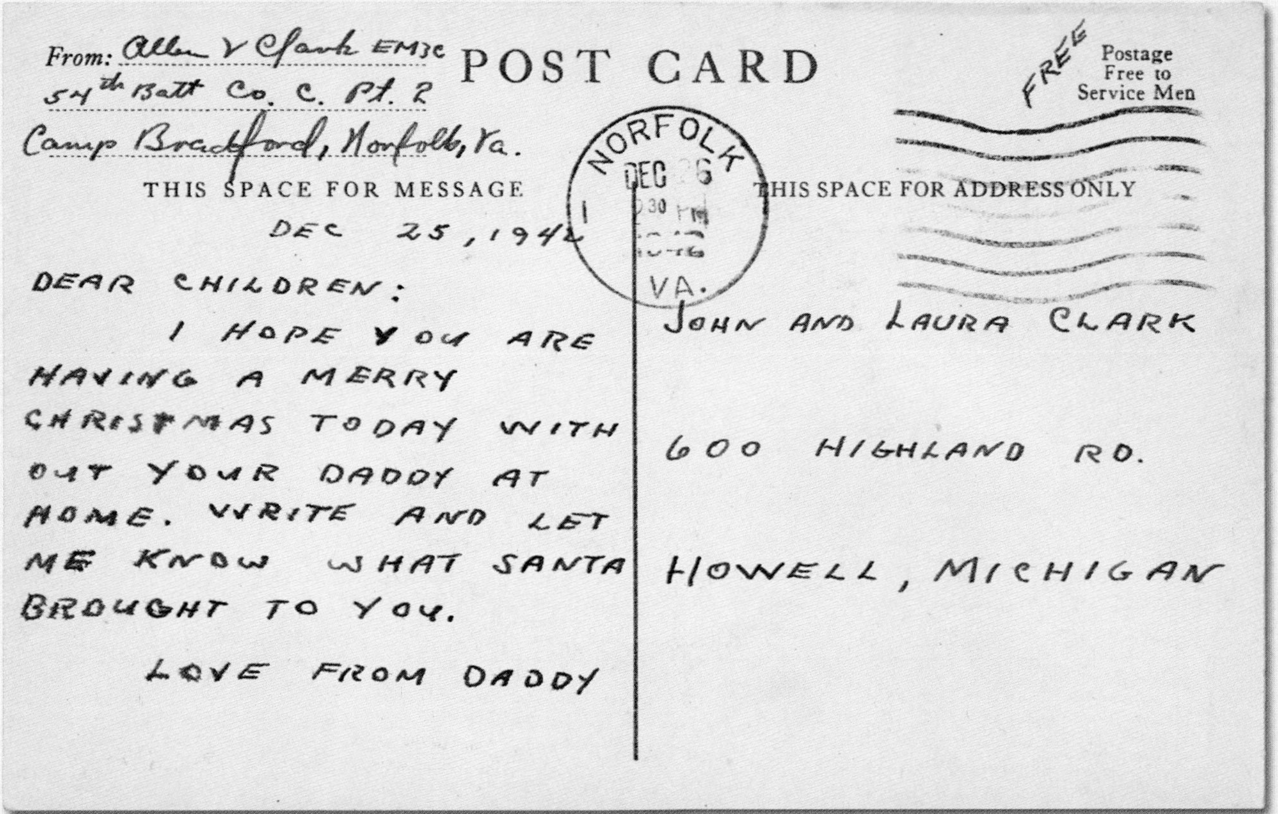

From: Allen V Clark EM3c
54th Batt Co. C. Pt. 2
Camp Bradford, Norfolk, Va.

POST CARD

FREE

Postage
Free to
Service Men

NORFOLK
DEC 26
30 PM
1942
VA.

THIS SPACE FOR MESSAGE

DEC 25, 1942

THIS SPACE FOR ADDRESS ONLY

DEAR CHILDREN:
I HOPE YOU ARE
HAVING A MERRY
CHRISTMAS TODAY WITH
OUT YOUR DADDY AT
HOME. WRITE AND LET
ME KNOW WHAT SANTA
BROUGHT TO YOU.

LOVE FROM DADDY

JOHN AND LAURA CLARK

600 HIGHLAND RD.

HOWELL, MICHIGAN

Hello Honey

I am sorry I can't write because of duty keeps me busy. I'll explain when I see you. You can start preparing our wedding because I miss we shipped near here. I love you very much. See you first changed I get time to fick like home.

Love Phil

P. Caratozolo Co. A
U. S. C. G
Eatons neck
Recieves Station N.Y.

NATURAL VIEW
POST CARD

Miss Gussie Marino
184 Stanhope St,
B'klyn, N.Y.

THIS SIDE FOR CORRESPONDENCE

THIS SIDE FOR ADDRESS

PLACE
ONE CENT
STAMP
HERE
MADE IN U.S.A.

MADE BY THE TOMLIN ART COMPANY, NORTHPORT, LONG ISLAND, N.Y.

GREETING ART
TOMLIN
CARDS

In January of 1943, when President Franklin Roosevelt and Prime Minister Winston Churchill met at Casablanca, in French Morocco, Roosevelt pledged that the Allies would fight until Germany had "unconditionally surrendered." Within a month, Soviet forces had broken the siege at Leningrad and accepted the surrender of the remaining Germans at Stalingrad. In retrospect, these events turned the tide of the European war. After February, the seemingly unbeatable Germans were constantly in retreat, and Russian forces would re-enter Poland by year's end.

During 1943, the enormous military and economic strength of the United States began to be felt on every battlefront. In the Pacific, after the U.S. forces won the fight for Guadalcanal in January, they began taking over the other Japanese-occupied islands. By the end of the year, they were in effective bombing range of Japan itself. Advancing in both directions across North Africa, the Allies took Tunisia, and then invaded Sicily in July. The joint American-British action precipitated the fall of Mussolini, and in early September, a new Italian government signed a peace treaty with the Allies. But German troops marched into Rome, established lines of defense, and held up the Allied advance north of Naples. It would be another ten months before the Allies reached Rome.

Nevertheless, victory now seemed more certain, and from late November until early December, Roosevelt, Stalin, and Churchill held their first meeting in Tehran. They discussed the Anglo-American invasion of Germany and plans for postwar cooperation.

On the American home front, support for the war continued to intensify. Vast numbers of factories that were largely employed by women were in full swing. "Rosie the Riveter" and "Wanda the Welder" became icons of aircraft manufacturing and assembly-line techniques. Determined factory workers clocked an average of fifty hours a week while maintaining the highest quality standards. They worked diligently, knowing that the weapons and any other equipment they turned out might be used by their husbands or brothers or sons—and must not fail.

The government worked constantly to maintain the country's enthusiastic spirit. An intense war bond campaign appealed to the patriots to "back the attack" by buying bonds, and over $100 billion worth were sold by 1945. To better finance the war effort, the system of withholding taxes on earned wages was instituted. The government also promoted scrap drives for critical materials—

metal and rubber in particular—that were in short supply and necessary for military use. Children, eager to make their patriotic contributions, supported these drives with great zeal. Because the country's farmers were too busy growing vegetables and fruits for the military, everyone was encouraged to plant "victory gardens" in every spot available. Many Americans lived in fear of invasion by the Germans or Japanese. To prepare for this possibility, communities throughout the country set up civil defense programs, which readied local citizens against possible enemy attack. Over 12 million volunteers participated in these programs.

War caused great transformations within American society. After an initial panic in 1942, Americans realized they were not in danger of invasion, but new racial hostilities were being felt. Japanese-Americans remained in prison camps, "zoot suit" rioters were repressed in California, and discrimination against Black Americans continued in both the military and at home. In spite of these tensions, audiences flocked to listen to such talented Black musical artists as Charlie Parker and Dizzy Gillespie, who rocked the nation with their revolutionary music.

Movies continued to be the most popular form of mass entertainment. During 1943, the country enjoyed such war classics as *Destination Tokyo, Watch on the Rhine,* and *Guadalcanal Diary,* while Mickey Rooney and Judy Garland provided lighter movie fare with *Girl Crazy.* The Mills Brothers' uplifting recording of "Paper Doll" topped the charts, while Broadway's theatrical production of *Oklahoma* offered two of the year's most popular songs—"Oh, What a Beautiful Mornin'" and "People Will Say We're in Love." On the literary scene, the country's growing optimism was reflected in such books as *A Tree Grows in Brooklyn, The Fountainhead,* and *My Native Land.*

In 1943, the battlefield had started to favor the Allies, and America's spirit began to soar. There was a glimmer of light at the end of war's dark tunnel. ✍

On the fashion front, the sale of women's pants—a practical result of women entering the work force—quadrupled in 1943 from the previous year.

125—"End of the Hike," Camp Blanding, Fla.

Pvt. M. Varano, 123rd Sig. Rad. Int. Co.
Camp Blanding, Florida

Dear Ma,

I got the stamps - for which thanks. I'm still waiting for my new suit. I'll let you know as soon as I get it.

Can you find me on the other side of the card? Don't look too hard because I'm not on there! See the kind of barracks we live in? No stoves now! Mich

POST CARD

Mrs. C. Varano
175 E. 22d St.
Holland, Mich.

CAMP BLANDING
JAN 28
3 PM
1943
FLA.

PLACE ONE CENT STAMP HERE
Free

DUVAL NEWS COMPANY, JACKSONVILLE, FLA.

GENUINE CURTEICH-CHICAGO "C.T. ART-COLORTONE" POST CARD (REG. U.S. PAT. OFF.)

Student Barrack No.   Chanute Field, Rantoul, Illinois

PHOTO BY U. S. ARMY AIR CORPS

1B-H1134

Hi folks, 2-21-43.

I am fine & well.
just a cards few lines,
I drove to day on range
& drive a 4,000 gal
tank of gasoline. What
a job. I love it. Grant
rate on Thurs, & Ships
on Fri. It's warm to-
day & beautiful out.
More later —
Love Pvt. Geo.
xx Clark

Thank U

POST CARD

PLACE
ONE CENT
STAMP
HERE

RANTOUL, ILL.
FEB 22
9:30 AM
1943

Dr. & Mrs. Clark
3560 E. 154 st.
Cleveland,
Ohio.

GENUINE CURTEICH-CHICAGO "C.T. ART-COLORTONE" POST CARD (REG. U.S. PAT. OFF.)

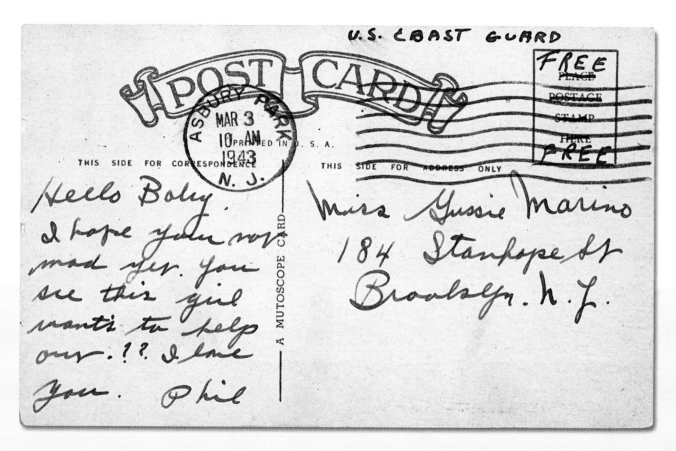

U.S. COAST GUARD

POST CARD

ASBURY PARK
MAR 3
10 AM
1943
N.J.

PRINTED IN U.S.A.

THIS SIDE FOR CORRESPONDENCE

THIS SIDE FOR ADDRESS ONLY

FREE
PLACE
POSTAGE
STAMP
HERE
FREE

— A MUTOSCOPE CARD —

Hello Baby.
I hope you not
mad yet. You
see this girl
wants to help
our.!? I love
you. Phil

Miss Gussie Marino
184 Stanhope St
Brooklyn. N.Y.

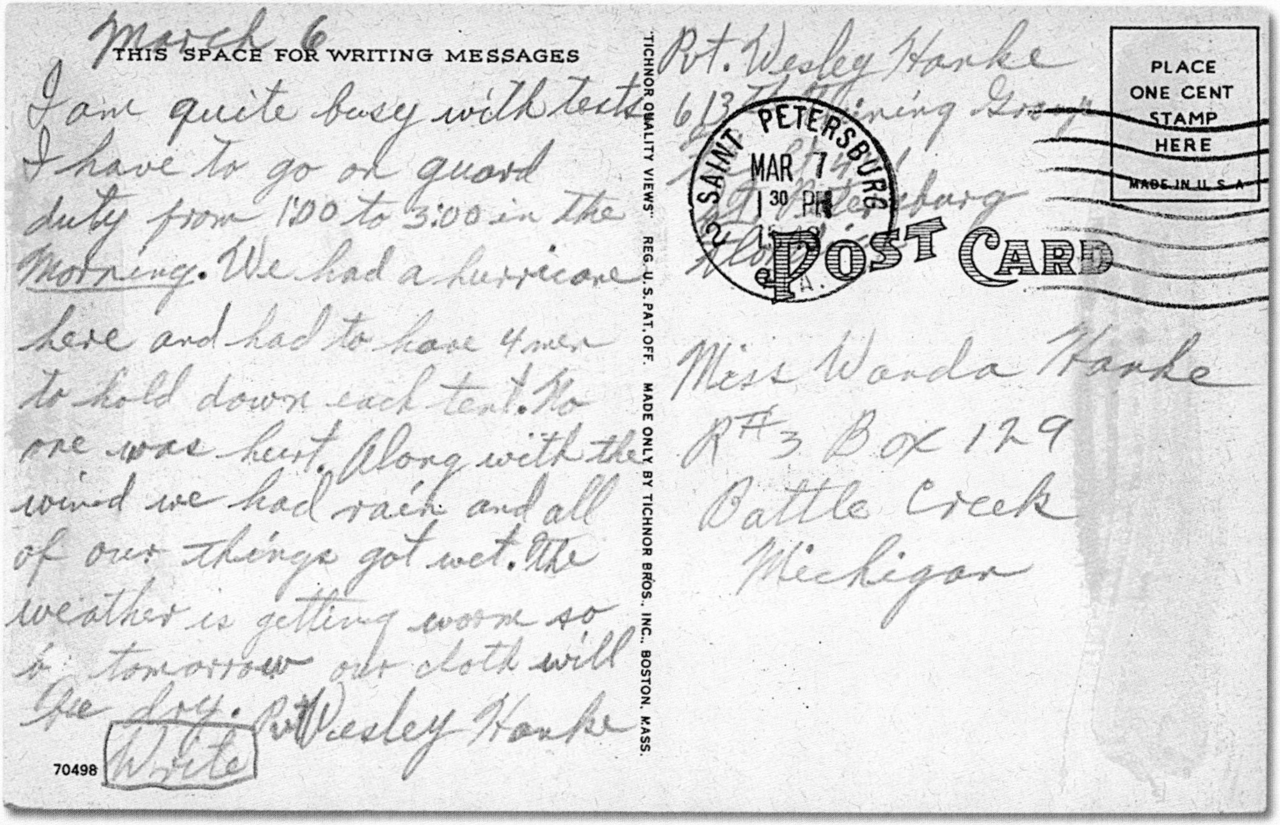

March 6

THIS SPACE FOR WRITING MESSAGES

I am quite busy with tests I have to go on guard duty from 1:00 to 3:00 in the morning. We had a hurricane here and had to have 4 men to hold down each tent. No one was hurt. Along with the wind we had rain and all of our things got wet. The weather is getting warm so tomorrow our cloth will be dry. Pvt Wesley Hanke

Write

70498

"TICHNOR QUALITY VIEWS" REG. U.S. PAT. OFF. MADE ONLY BY TICHNOR BROS., INC., BOSTON, MASS.

Pvt. Wesley Hanke
613th Training Group
Florida

SAINT PETERSBURG MAR 7 1 30 PM FLA.

POST CARD

PLACE ONE CENT STAMP HERE MADE IN U.S.A.

Miss Wanda Hanke
R#3 Box 129
Battle Creek
Michigan

Troops Moving Out For Morning Drill

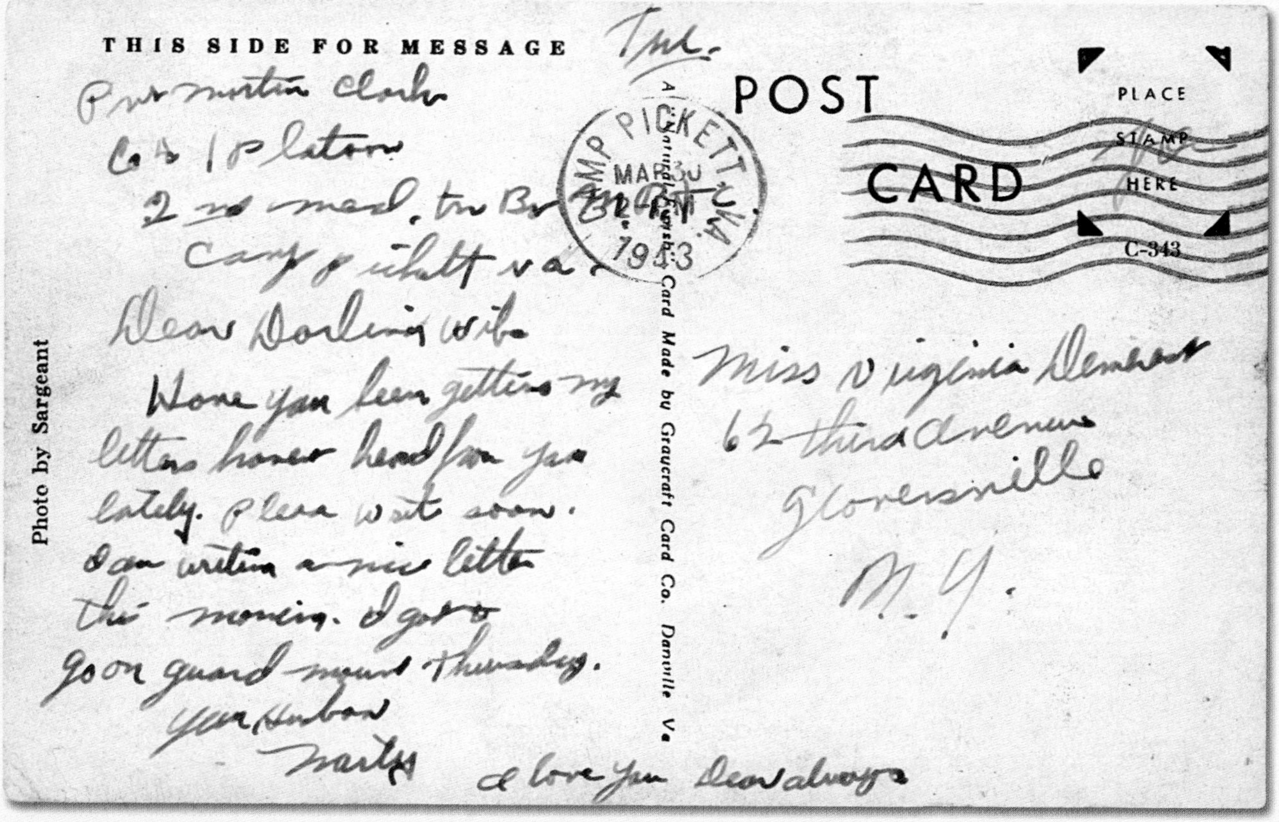
THIS SIDE FOR MESSAGE

Tml.

Pvt Morton Clark
Co A 1 platoon
2 nd med. tr Bn
Camp Pickett Va.

Dear Darling wife

Have you been getting my letters haven't heard from you lately. please write soon. I am writing a nice letter this morning. I got to go on guard mount Thursday.

Your Husband
Marty

I love you dear always

Photo by Sargeant

A Natural Finish Card Made by Graucraft Card Co. Danville Va.

CAMP PICKETT, VA.
MAR 30
1943

POST CARD

PLACE STAMP HERE

C-343

Miss Virginia Demhart
62 third Avenue
Gloversville
N.Y.

Jeep in Action at Fort Custer, Michigan

73792

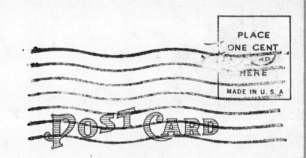

PVT LAURENCE J LEACH
Co. C 1604 S.U.
BRKS. 1044
FORT CUSTER, MICH

THIS SPACE FOR WRITING MESSAGES

Hi Jim,
SORRY I COULDN'T TALK LONGER
ON THE PHONE BUT I WILL
CALL ⬛ SOME OTHER TIME.
HOW IS DAISY? IT IS RAINING
HERE. THIS PICTURE IS NATURAL
AROUND HERE. THOSE JEEPS
HIT A BUMP & JUMP ABOUT
6 FT INTO THE AIR. WELL
SO LONG FOR NOW.
            LARRY   SUN. APRIL 4

PUB. BY STEVENSON CAMERA SHOP, BATTLE CREEK, MICH.

"TICHNOR QUALITY VIEWS". REG. U.S. PAT. OFF. MADE ONLY BY TICHNOR BROS., INC. BOSTON, MASS.

BATTLE CREEK
APR 5
4³⁰ PM
2 1943
MICH.

POST CARD

PLACE
ONE CENT
HERE
MADE IN U.S.A.

MR. JAMES LEACH
1570 HADLEY RD.
LAPEER,
MICH

Keeping in Touch

Sixteen million Americans served in the armed forces during WWII, and for the vast majority, the most important part of any day was mail call. Letters and postcards were the "care packages" that connected servicemen to home.

Despite the difficulty of transporting letters and packages to foreign locations, mail constituted a vital part of the war effort. In 1943, the average soldier received fourteen pieces of mail each week. Even soldiers without family got mail from the many "pen pals" who made it part of their daily routine to write. And every combatant received a personal letter from President Roosevelt telling him of the essential job he was doing. The government also contributed. During the war, it published tiny paperback editions of books—forty titles a month—which were distributed to soldiers on every front. But for the GIs, mail primarily meant letters from home. For many servicemen, letters from friends and loved ones became an obsession, and army psychiatrists were always on the alert for those who allowed mail (or the lack of it) to control their lives. Themes of many stories and soap operas revolve around the traumas resulting from "Dear John" letters, called "green bananas" by Pacific fighters. But most mail kept up the spirits of the fighting forces. It let them know that the home front was thinking of them and praying for their return.

Soldiers were also encouraged to write home, although boot-camp trainees were often too tired to write at the end of their sixteen-hour days, and, obviously, those in active combat situations simply couldn't. In general, however, when combat troops left their ships, the men had written more than a dozen letters apiece. It was this huge volume of mail that led to the government's creation of V-mail in an effort to save space and weight. After they were censored, personal letters that were written by servicemen were photographed. The film was then

Mail call was the high point of a soldier's day, but it was rare in combat zones. In 1943, the average soldier received fourteen pieces of mail each week.

processed, and the letters—in a reduced size—were printed on 4-x-5.5 inch cards. Thanks to this process, letters weighing slightly over 2,500 pounds were greatly reduced to a weight of slightly less than 50 pounds. Many, however, didn't appreciate the entire V-mail process, as it replaced a letter with something that resembled a postcard. But over a billion of these messages were sent during the conflict, and most arrived at their destinations within ten days.

One problem with mail came from the existence of an Office of Censorship in a nation fighting for the right of free speech. The OC had power over all foreign mail, as well as films, radio, and print publications. Censorship was so complete during the war that the President once took an 8,754-mile trip around the nation and not a single word appeared in any newspaper. Moreover, it was not until late in 1943 that a single picture of a dead GI was permitted to be published. In 1941, the Attorney General authorized the censoring of every soldier's letters. Soldiers knew and understood that their officers would censor missives from the battlefront, but most felt that opening their domestic letters was excessive.

Even when blackened by the censor's pen, the billions of letters, V-mail cards, and postcards sent during the war confirmed the beliefs and values for which the nation was fighting. Mail call represented the strongest connection between fighting men and the home front. Whether read on an Aleutian Island or a Pacific atoll, behind a French hedgerow or on Main Street, USA, written correspondence between Americans lifted the spirits and reinforced the commitment of a united people.

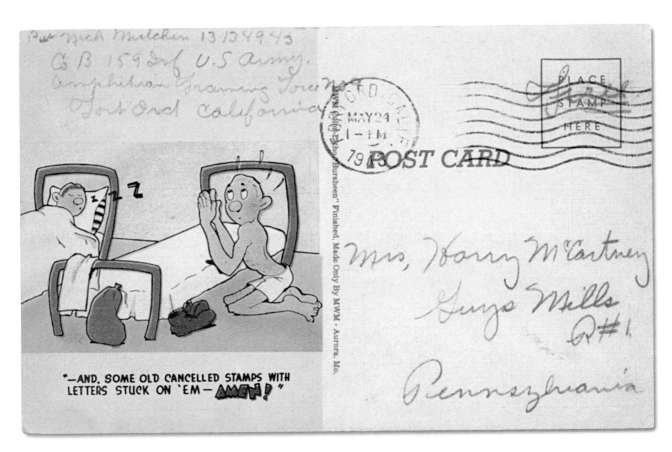

Hellow Neighbor,
I am well
& hope you are th
same its been warm
here & ther is one thing
that is really funny
about this place you sweat
like heck in th sun
but when you sit in the
shade of a tree you dog-
on near freeze believe me
that is th truth.
if ther is any news
of back home pleasetell
to route it your
good friend &
neighbor
Pat Nicholas

THIS SPACE FOR WRITING MESSAGES

Hi Elda,
I wonder if you will still
be in Cleveland when Ben Ames
gets there. Are you going to
keep the canteen open at all
during the summer? If not,
how about sending me
your home address, so that
I can reform, and write to
you now and then.
How did you make out in
your course? At least a
B, I'll bet.
Johnny

70321

Pvt. J. D. Velando
Sqn. 466-601 T.C.
63rd Tc. Wing
Clearwater, Florida

CLEARWATER
JUN 4
1945

POST CARD

Miss Elda Beery
1710 Prospect Avenue
Cleveland, Ohio

FORT ORD, MONTEREY, CALIFORNIA—M21

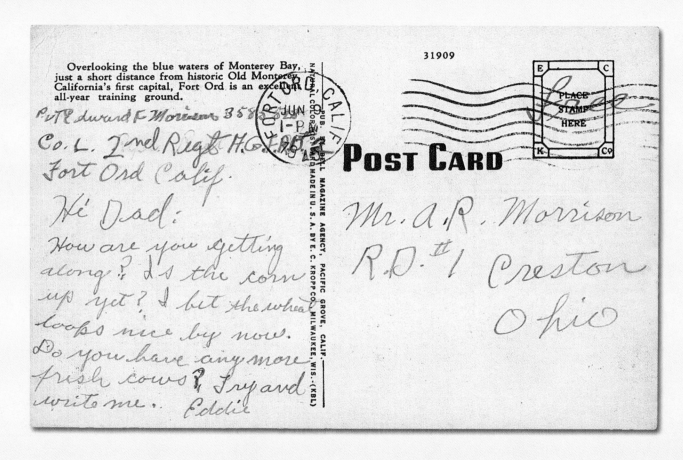

Overlooking the blue waters of Monterey Bay,
just a short distance from historic Old Monterey,
California's first capital, Fort Ord is an excellent
all-year training ground.

31909

POST CARD

Pvt Edward F Morrison 358...
Co. L. 2nd Regt H.C...
Fort Ord Calif.

Hi Dad:
How are you getting
along? Is the corn
up yet? I bet the wheat
looks nice by now.
Do you have any more
fresh cows? Try and
write me.
Eddie

PUB. BY ALL NATL MAGAZINE AGENCY, PACIFIC GROVE, CALIF. — NATURAL COLOR PHOTO AND MADE IN U. S. A. BY E. C. KROPP CO., MILWAUKEE, WIS.—(KBL)

Mr. A. R. Morrison
R.D. #1 Creston
Ohio

A/c R. L. Poehlmann, AAFPFS (B-N)
Sqdn A-1, Class 43-17, Selman Field
Monroe, La.

Brad:

These are the type of planes I'll be training in several weeks when I get to advanced. Pre-Flight is nearing it's close now and I'm doing swell. Give my regards to Claire and the boys of #324

Bob.

FREE

1c
STAMP
U.S.A.
POSTAGE

Post Card

MONROE, LA. 7
JUN 28
5 30 PM
7943

MR. JOHN L. BRADFORD

929 FAUNCE ST.

PHILADELPHIA,

PENNA.

Jumbo Post Card Co.—San Antonio, Texas

Snowy slopes of the Rocky Mountains are the textbook for a group of navigation cadets on a routine training flight from the Army Air Forces Navigation School, Selman Field, La. Cadets in this twin-motored AT-7 navigation training ship may some future day guide a U. S. Flying Fortress on a bombing mission over uncharted enemy territory.

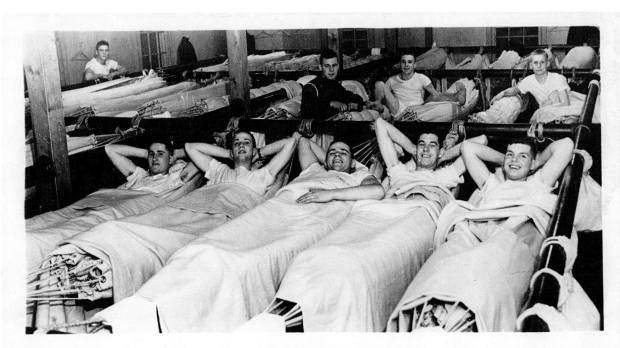

Boys in Hammocks
U. S. NAVAL TRAINING STATION, GREAT LAKES, ILLINOIS
REAR ADMIRAL, JOHN DOWNES U.S. NAVY, COMMANDING OFFICER

POST CARD

CORRESPONDENCE

ADDRESS ONLY

Marion Nauszelski
co 914 U.S.N.T.
Great Lakes, Ill.
July 16, 1943
9:30 P.M.

Dear Alice,

I haven't heard from you this week. Is there anything wrong? I got another shot in my arm today. Boy! is it killing me. I am going to sleep now. With love a good night to you.

Mike

Free

JUL 17
4 PM
1943

Miss Alice Danaj
Cross Village
Michigan

U. S. Army Pursuit Plane (Bell Airacobra P-39)

THIS SIDE FOR MESSAGE

POST CARD

PLACE STAMP HERE

F-196

Photograph Courtesy Bell Aircraft Corp.

A "Natural Finish" Card Made by Graycraft Card Co., Danville, Va.

P.F.C. Romaine L. Hugh
10th Photo. Sqd.
Peterson Field
Colorado Springs, Colo.

Dear Lydia

Would have written
sooner but am quite
busy. A hailstorm
destroyed my garden.
I am O.K. Just a
little lonesome. Sure
is hot out here. Sure
like the papers. Thanks.
Hope you folks are
all O.K. Love "Bill"

Mrs. Lydia Cimons
1228 Hickory St.
Lansing 15
Michigan.

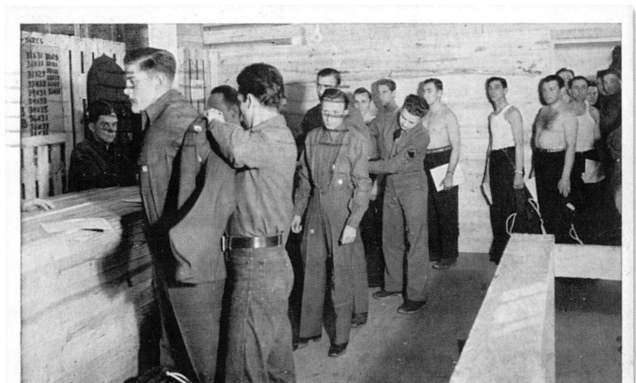

Re. C. 4   Reception Center—Being Fitted with Blouses and Trousers.   *Greetings from New Cumberland, Pa.*

From: Pvt Nicholas Bocko
Co. C. Roster 2826
1301 St. Service Unit
New Cumberland Pa.

33 82 9756 U.S. Army

POST CARD
THIS SPACE FOR ADDRESS ONLY

THIS SPACE FOR MESSAGE

Hi Pal
How's everything
with you. I got my
Uniform. I Be leaving
for camp. Soon.
I'll write sooner.
Pal
Good Luck Nick

Claude Santos
East Bangor
Penna.

FOR VICTORY
BUY
UNITED
STATES
WAR
BONDS
AND
STAMPS

W. R. THOMPSON & COMPANY, PUBLISHERS, RICHMOND, VIRGINIA

NEW CUMBERLAND
AUG 6
1 PM
1943
PA.

Orders to Move On
U.S. NAVAL TRAINING STATION, GREAT LAKES, ILLINOIS

POST CARD

CORRESPONDENCE   ADDRESS

GREAT LAKES
AUG 22
10³⁰ AM
1943
ILL.

Ship Service Stores - Great Lakes, Inc.

GPO

Donald Irwin Hess AS
Company #1138
U.S.N.T.S.
Great Lake, Ill.

Dea Mil;
Sure hope we
get these orders
soon. I _ _ _ _ this
place.
Don

Mrs Donald Hess
227 South Hartley St
York,
Penna

Feeding the G.I.s

The extraordinary rigors of World War II exerted great pressure on the military's food supply. Meeting the nutritional needs of the tremendous numbers of soldiers who were involved in combat and assault operations proved a significant challenge. At the beginning of the war, the Army had two types of field rations—"emergency" D-rations and "food-for-a day" C-rations—that had been developed earlier. These supplemental food supplies were designed to sustain a soldier's nutritional needs during those times when he was cut off from regular food sources.

The D-ration was a four-ounce, vitamin-fortified "power bar" made primarily of chocolate, sugar, and oat flour. Developed by Colonel Paul P. Logan and sometimes referred to as a *Logan bar,* each unit contained 600 calories and was intended for use as an emergency food. It was to be eaten slowly, or dissolved in a cup of boiling water and drunk. The C-ration was to serve as a three-meal-a day food source; it included canned meat, biscuits, sugar, and powdered coffee, which were consolidated in a large can.

C- and D-rations, although useful, were unable to meet many of the unique problems imposed by the war. The D-ration was intended only as a supplement to relieve the hunger of a single missed meal, and the C-ration was simply too heavy and bulky for mobile units. This necessitated the development of rations with superior content and packaging.

In 1941, prior to the U.S. entry into the war, Dr. Ancel B. Keyes, physiologist and Director of the Laboratory of Physiological Hygiene at the University of Minnesota, was commissioned by the government to help develop a nutritionally packed meal for troops in combat. Additional concern had to be given to stability and storage requirements, as well as weight, size, and packaging

Despite heartfelt complaints about C-rations, D-rations, and K-rations, the American fighting man was the best-fed soldier of World War II.

specifications. Wartime shortages of materials added to the challenge. The result was the K-ration—a 3,000-calorie, three-meal unit that was packaged initially in a lightweight plastic-coated carton.

Although the K-ration was an immediate success, developers continued to improve both its contents and packaging during the war years. A variety of newer, more palatable meat products was added, as were assorted crackers and biscuits. Small two-ounce D-bars were often included; however, other candies eventually made their way into the packs. In addition to instant coffee, powdered beverages like fruit drinks, cocoa, and malted milk were offered. Nonfood "accessory" items including cigarettes, matches, chewing gum, toilet paper, and eating utensils were standard, as were salt tablets to help alleviate heat exhaustion.

A typical K-ration breakfast often consisted of a can of chopped ham and eggs, two types of biscuits, a fruit bar, instant coffee, sugar cubes, and a small D-ration bar. Lunch units included items like canned American cheese or ham spread, biscuits, malted milk tablets, and powdered lemon drink. Beef stew, veal, and spaghetti and meatballs were common items found in the dinner packs, along with bouillon powder, instant coffee, peanuts, and raisins.

The three individual meals came in separate containers marked breakfast, lunch, and dinner, and were then packaged in one larger carton. Packaging was as important as the food itself. The containers, which continued to improve over time, had to be durable enough to withstand possible temperatures as high as 135 degrees and as low as minus 20. They also had to be waterproof. Eventually, sturdy wax-coated cardboard containers were found to be the most suitable.

During 1944, over 105 million K-rations were produced. By the end of the war, however, they began taking a back seat to new and improved C-rations, and in 1946, they were discontinued altogether. The value of K-rations during the war years cannot be denied—they offered the best food available in the most convenient packaging for the country's fighting soldiers in the field.

The Navy urged American boys to
"Choose While You Can," and skimmed
off some of the best volunteers—but
perhaps a few regretted the decision?

ABANDON SHIP DRILL
U.S. Naval Training Station
Great Lakes, Ill.

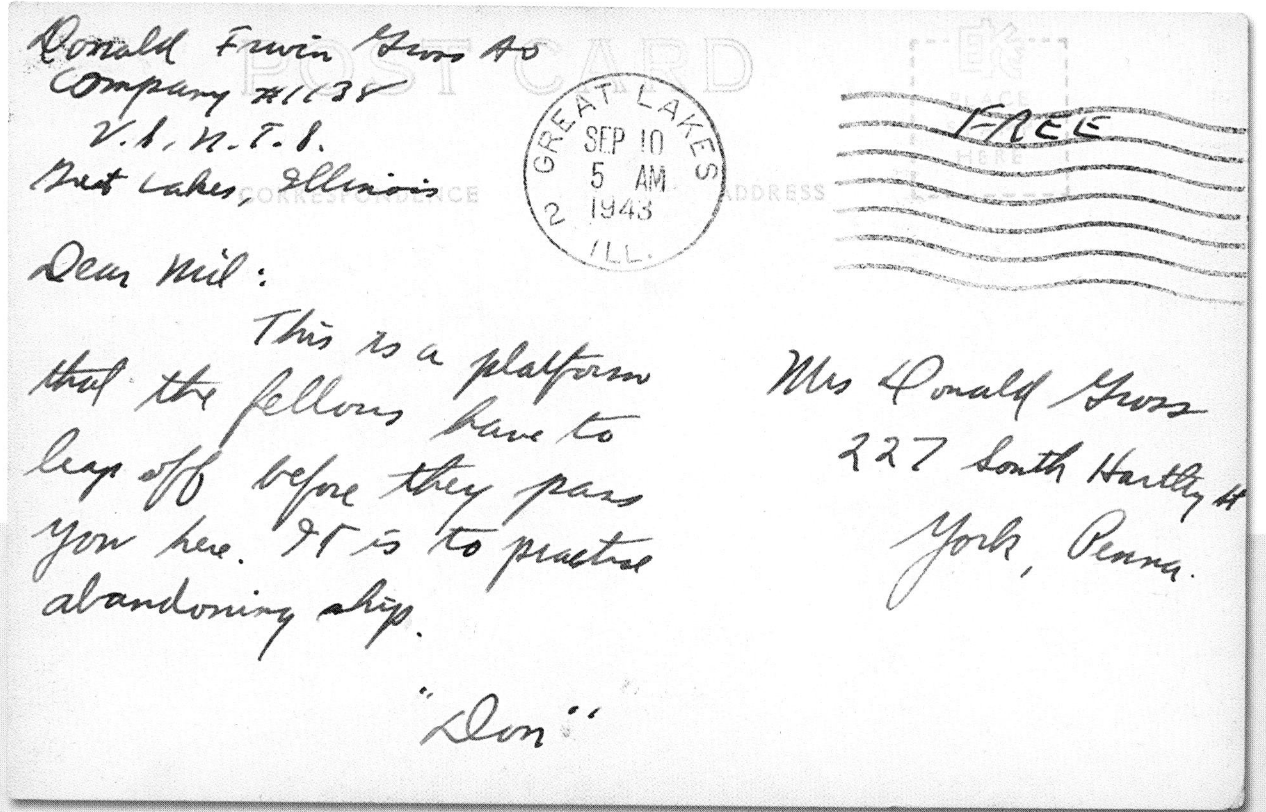

POST CARD

Donald Erwin Gross AS
Company #1138
U.S.N.T.S.
Great Lakes, Illinois

CORRESPONDENCE

GREAT LAKES
SEP 10
5 AM
1943
2
ILL.

ADDRESS

PLACE STAMP HERE

FREE

Dear Mil:

This is a platform that the fellows have to leap off before they pass you here. It is to practise abandoning ship.

"Don"

Mrs Donald Gross
227 South Hartley St
York, Penna.

PASSING SHELLS TO LOADER
U. S. NAVY

OFFICIAL U.S. NAVY PHOTOGRAPH

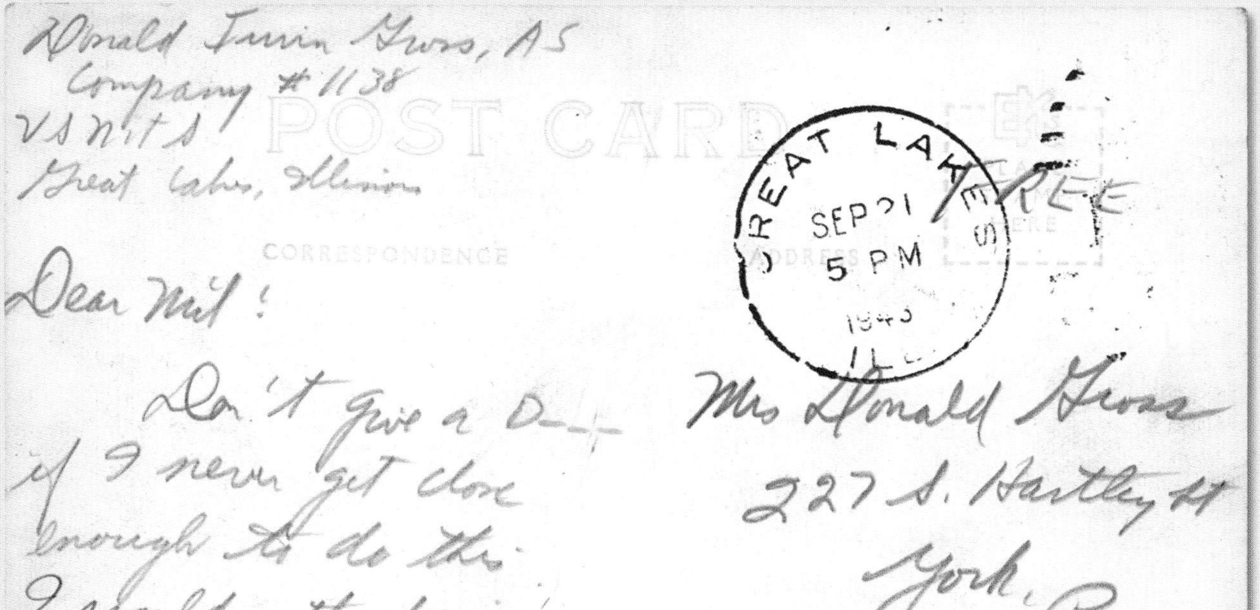

Donald Irwin Gross, AS
Company #1138
U S N T S
Great Lakes, Illinois

POST CARD

CORRESPONDENCE

REAT LAKES
SEP 21
5 PM
1943
ILL

FREE

Dear Mil!

Don't give a D--- if I never get close enough to do this I would rather be in the Home Guards.

Love

Don

ADDRESS

Mrs Donald Gross
227 S. Hartley St
York, Penna

ANCHORED
U S N
TO
DEMOCRACY
MOLE

U. S. NAVAL TRAINING STATION,
GREAT LAKES, ILLINOIS
REAR ADMIRAL, JOHN DOWNES U S NAVY,
COMMANDING OFFICER

By 1945, the Navy had 105 carriers, 5,000 ships and submarines, and 82,000 other vessels.

James E. Cassidy A-S.
U.S.N.T.S. Co. 1495
Great Lakes, Ill.

CORRESPONDENCE

Dear Mother & Dad
I am ok but kinda
lonesome. So drop me
a line now and then
Hope you are both ok
When you write use the
address at the top of the
card. Love from gene
Son Jim

FREE

GREAT LAKES
OCT 5
5 AM
1943
ILL.

Mr & Mrs Wm Cassidy
800 Robinwood St.
Pontiac, Mich.

Hello Jerk,

Feeling Fine
Steve. Getting my
Furlogh in this
week or next for
sure. Getting married
on my Furlogh. Berta
getting married on 26th
of Oct. Churches is my
usher. Don't forget
to come Steve. Ill be
waiting. Your Pal
Johnny.

MWM Color-Litho Postcards Made Only By MWM - Aurora. Mo.

SPARTANBURG
OCT 19
9 AM
1943
S. C.

Pvt J. Mostanovsky
33673885
32nd, Infan. Bn,
Co. D 3rd Plat.
Camp croft S. C.

Free

POST CARD

Pvt. S. Broskovich
Co. L, 3rd Bn, 176 th,
Ft. Benning,
Ga,

Hello Lloyd;
    Having a good
time working
day nite.
    I'm in charge
of the mess-hall
now. Hope you
are well and getting
along alright, Bro.
rationing on liquors
out this way come
on out. your Bro.
        Glenn J. Lewis

P. F. C. G. J. Lewis
A.S.N. 36861875
Co B 73 rd Engrs
Camp Beale, Calif

Joel

CAMP BEALE
OCT 26
CALIF.

POST CARD

STAMP
HERE

GRAYCRAFT CARD CO. DANVILLE, VA.

Mr Lloyd W. Lewis
Milner Hotel
119 N. Main St.
Ann Arbor
    Michigan

In May of 1944, Allied forces in Italy drove the Germans out of Monte Cassino, and finally opened the way for the liberation of all Italy; Rome was taken on June 4. In May, the Germans surrendered in Crimea, and the Red Army continued driving the Germans from the huge Leningrad salient. All of this was but a prelude to the Anglo-American invasion of France on D-Day, June 6, 1944. Operation Overlord landed in Normandy, France, and initiated the most important battle on Europe's western front. The film *Saving Private Ryan* recreates this historic event, and serves as a testament to the tremendous numbers of lives that were sacrificed before the Allies were victorious.

On August 25, Paris was liberated, but Hitler had one last card to play. In December, his remaining panzer units, supported by boys as young as fourteen years old, counterattacked in a weakly guarded area of the Ardennes Forest on the Belgian-German border. The all-out surprise attack, which ultimately involved over a million men, was the largest land battle of the war. It was known as the Battle of the Bulge because the Germans initially succeeded in causing a "bulge" in the American front lines. The American victory in January of 1945 greatly reduced Germany's ability to resist invasion.

Meanwhile, in the Pacific, the island-hopping campaigns had successfully reduced Japan's area of operations and made possible General Douglas MacArthur's return to the Philippines in October. Late that month, American naval forces decisively defeated the remainder of Japan's surface fleet and kamikazi pilots in the Battle of Leyte Gulf, the greatest naval engagement of all time. The year ended with B-29 attacks on Tokyo itself. Clearly, the conflict was rapidly coming to a conslusion.

At home, the devastating cost of victory—the loss of fathers and sons, brothers and sisters—was all too apparent. Star-bearing banners hung in the front windows of homes throughout the country. Each blue star signified a family member who was in active service; yellow stars represented those who had died. With 12 million people in the service, everyone knew someone who was fighting in the war, a fact that caused nervous apprehension whenever the doorbell rang. Yet, the country's solidarity never wavered. The cause had always been viewed as a fight between good and evil, a battle in which democracy had to defeat fascism.

By 1944, women constituted nearly 40 percent of the country's workforce. Not only did they make up the bulk of the workers on factory assembly lines, but they also drove trucks, pumped gas, and performed other jobs once held by men. They also found time to manage traditional household chores. Yet, despite their services, women were not treated equally in their paychecks. The average weekly salary for a woman in 1944 was $31.21; for a man, it was $54.65.

As always, some of the money that was made during the war was spent going to the movies. *Double Indemnity* was one of the year's classic thrillers, while *The Miracle of Morgan's Creek* offered audiences a comic wartime farce. *Thirty Seconds Over Tokyo* gave an account of the first American attack on Japan—the Doolittle Raid of April 1942. On the music scene, Johnny Mercer's popular "Accentuate the Positive" was one of the year's most uplifting tunes. It lent supportive words to a country whose people lived through the war each day.

Keeping a stiff upper lip was necessary, for the toll of battle was apparent in long casualty lists. Each day, people opened their morning papers to discover the names of those who had been killed during the most recent fighting. The sight of Western Union couriers delivering much-dreaded telegrams became an all too familiar sight. Americans everywhere had sacrificed for the war. By the end of 1944, they felt confident that their dreams of peace were about to be fulfilled. ॐ

U.S. Fifth Army Ducks Beachhead near Anzio, Italy - 1944
Courtesy U.S. Army Photo

The development of invasion craft and beachhead landings was a great tactical achievement of the United States during World War II.

Pfc. Harvey R. Carpenter, 36462589
Squadron 41 F.A.F.R.D.
Hammer Field, Fresno, Calif.

Dear Folks,
        I got here about
four o'clock this morning.
I was four hours late.
Don't expect to be here
long. I am living
in a tent. Dolly and
I didn't get married.
It is raining out here.
I will tell you more
when I write a letter.
        love. Harvey.

Mrs Clarence Welbourn
Yale, Michigan

POST CARD

WESTERN PUBLISHING & NOVELTY CO., LOS ANGELES, CALIF.

"C.T. ART-COLORTONE" REG. U.S. PAT. OFF.

PLACE
ONE CENT
STAMP
HERE

FRESNO
FEB 22
7:30 PM
1944
CALIF.

WEST GATE TO TYNDALL FIELD NEAR PANAMA CITY, FLORIDA

121-P

STOP

PHOTO BY SOUTHEAST
AIR FORCES TRAINING
CENTER, TYNDALL FIELD, FLA.

THIS SPACE FOR WRITING MESSAGES

The Dothan Cigar & Candy Company, Panama City, Florida

COPY PICTURE PUBLICATION, CAMBRIDGE, MASS. U.S.A.

PANAMA CITY FLA
PM
APR 28
1944

POST CARD

UNITED STATES POSTAGE
GEORGE WASHINGTON
1 CENT 1

A VISIT TO THE DOWN HERE
HOW MANY CASES DO YOU WANT
FRANK + THELMA LOOK SWELL
BUT FRANK LOST EIGHT LBS.
BUT FEELS GOOD NOW. BOY
WERE THEY GLAD TO SEE
ME. THEY ARE STAYING AT A
SWELL HOME. UNCLE BITZ.

STEAK AC COSTS $1.10

Schafer's
Tavern
Genesee Road
Alden
N.Y.

THIS SPACE FOR WRITING MESSAGES

FREE

PLACE
ONE CENT
STAMP
HERE

POST CARD

PUBLICATION CAMBRIDGE, MASS. U.S.A.

Hi, Ma.

This card is just
off the serious side.
I took my classification
tests yesterday and
got all high marks.
Way above average.
They wanted to make me
a radioman but you
have to have three years
of typing which I
haven't had. Will write
later.   Andy

Mrs. Bertha Andrews
124 A Marianna St.
East Lynn
Mass.

Seabees at Sea and at Disembarkation Point, Greeting from Camp Perry, Va *U. S. Navy Photo*

1625—"Seabees aboard transport with full
equipment bound for active duty. Dis-
embarking at advanced base."

Clark Bastress, MM
Area B-9 SR. Plt.5
Camp Peary, VA.

POST CARD
THIS SPACE FOR ADDRESS ONLY

S. NAVY
MAY 1
3-PM
1944

SEABEES

Hello Folks; how's
the world treating you
by this time? I hope
your all in good shape.
I am OK but give me
time any old time. We've
kept pretty busy down
here. But the chow is pretty
good.

Your Bro-in-law
Clark B.

THIS SPACE FOR MESSAGE

Mr. & Mrs. Russell Young,
Northumberland
R.D. #1,
PA.

Images of the Times

By 1944, posters supporting the war effort had become an integral part of American life. They could be seen hanging practically everywhere—in schools, banks, railway stations, factories, restaurants, and store windows. Some were as small as a sheet of writing paper, while others were as big as highway road signs. Their messages were simple and direct: conserve resources, work hard, buy savings bonds, be patriotic, be careful who you speak to, and remember that your Uncle Sam still wants you. With stirring, often haunting images and inspirational slogans, posters were constant reminders that the country was at war.

The use of posters as a means of promotion began at the turn of the nineteenth century with advances in the printing process. The ability to produce beautiful full-color posters inexpensively made them a highly successful way to advertise products or events. During World War I, posters were an effective means

Artist James Montgomery Flagg used his own face as the model for this recruiting poster—perhaps the most famous image of World War II.

Civilians working back home were essential to America's war effort; by 1945, the United States was creating half of the world's total product.

of stirring up patriotic fervor. After the war, the country's military branches continued using posters to encourage young men to enlist.

Within one week of the bombing of Pearl Harbor, the government began issuing posters that subtly reflected the changing times. Many of these first WWII posters were nothing more than altered reprints of the ones used during peacetime. Original copy had simply been rewritten to reflect the current "national emergency." Over the next several months, a number of governmental agencies began producing the first wave of original war posters. However, because of the wide overlap of responsibilities among these agencies, the Office of War Information, more commonly known as the OWI, was formed in June of 1942. Its purpose was to review and approve the design of posters from the various government groups, as well as to coordinate their production and distribution. The OWI was also responsible for producing posters of its own.

Francis Brennan, the former art director of *Fortune* magazine, was selected as the first chief of the OWI Graphics Division. With the goal of using contemporary

INDUSTRY · THE ARSENAL OF DEMOCRACY

RALPH ILIGAN

"... It is not the individual
Or the army as a whole,
But the everlastin' teamwork
Of every bloomin' soul."
J. MASON KNOX

"The Call to Defense is a Call to Us All"

World War II was a "good war" that united the nation as one; contributions of every citizen were valued.

advertising design elements to highlight the country's wartime needs and goals, Brennan quickly recruited talented artists from the best-known ad agencies to produce simple yet persuasive images.

Government agencies were not the only sources of war posters. Many businesses, including General Motors, Seagram, Western Union, and Abbott Laboratories, produced posters for the war effort, as did a number of trade associations, war relief agencies, and private individuals. Before the end of the war, such art luminaries as Norman Rockwell, James Montgomery Flagg, NC Wyeth, Ben Shahn, and Walt Disney had made poster contributions.

As a group, these posters—much like their postcard counterparts—provide a unique look at this period of our country's history. They mirror a nation that was intent on coming together to face an unparalleled challenge.

Images of the Times

Words such as "BROTHERHOOD," "SACRIFICE," and "VICTORY," emblazoned on posters in bold letters, were not solely intended to spur patriotism or play upon emotions. They were also meant to remind Americans that somewhere in the world, soldiers and sailors were fighting and dying for them, and that they needed to unite and stand behind them. Posters were a true reflection of the nation's resolve to win the war.

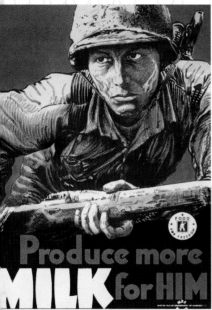

Produce more MILK for HIM

The images of soldiers in action were used to spur production throughout America's many industries.

We Can Do It

Women in the work force increased as much during World War II as in all of the years between 1900 and 1940.

May 4, 1944

THIS SPACE FOR WRITING MESSAGES

Morris H. Andrews A.S.
Co 413 U.S.N.T.C.
Sampson, N.Y

Just received your letter
today and also the 2(
you know what I mean).
You don't have to worry
about my coming home
because the train fare
to boston is taken out of
your pay and the tickets
bought for you so you
can expect me anytime
the last week of this month
See you soon Andy

POST CARD

Mrs. Bertha Andrews
124A Marianna St
East Lynn,
Mass.

FREE

PLACE
ONE CENT
STAMP
HERE

NAVY
MAY 5
11-AM

"COLOURPICTURE" PUBLICATION. CAMBRIDGE. MASS. U.S.

THIS SPACE FOR WRITING MESSAGES

NAME Pvt. A. RALPH NESTA 953008

RANK Plt. 328, 1st Rec. Bn. U.S.M.C.

PARRIS ISLAND, S.C.

UNITED STATES MARINE CORPS

Hi Folks; Believe it or not I'm
the "POP" of all the Marine Recruits
here on the "Island" and don't think
for a minute I don't feel like it.
What a setup. Tomorrow is our
first 20 mile hike I'm looking
forward to falling out and getting
a ride back to the Barracks—
        Regards to all
                Ralph

MARINE BKS.   FREE

POST CARD

        "Gven"

Mr. & Mrs. "Tony" Manupella
508 Third Ave. No.
Troy, New York

SCOUT TRAINER   Official U.S. Navy Photograph   Pub by Ellis 858

R.K. Judd A.M.M. 3/c
U.S.N.A.F.
Mt. Vernon, Wash.

June 1 1944

MOUNT VERNON
JUN 13
10 30 AM
1944
WASH.

free
U.S.N.

POST CARD

CORRESPONDENCE

ADDRESS

Dear Richie & Lesily.
here is an S.N.T. navy
scout trainer plane.
I am very sorry I couldn't
talk to you on the phone, but
I am going to call again at
your house. And early to.
I sure do miss you Richie. Don't
forget me now. Love Merle & Dich. X OXOX OX

Richard Kenneth Steiner
2712 Longview
Saginaw, Mich.

Clothing Warehouse

PHOTO COPYRIGHT BY F. M. KIRKPATRICK

Reception Center, Fort Benjamin Harrison, Indiana

2B415-N

Have arrived here Sunday and was surprised to see the terrific change taken place in my son. he is all from worry and frets to be here. all things that come in with him are gone about a week already.

Mrs A. O.

F. M. KIRKPATRICK, FT. BENJAMIN HARRISON, IND.

GENUINE CURTEICH-CHICAGO "C.T. AMERICAN ART" POST CARD

POST CARD

Mr & Mrs Warren Kobelt
R. D # 1
La Grange, Ohio.

GEORGE J. NOSIS %S COGST CAMP WALDRON
UNITED STATES NAVAL TRAINING STATION

FARRAGUT, IDAHO

CORRESPONDENCE

Hi Tony

How is the old man
getting along I hope you are
all right. Over here I'm just
fine. Tell ma that's me on
the other side. Tony don't
enlist in anything please
I am sorry myself so do
me that favor ok. I'll write
you a letter when I have
time. So long for now
P.S.   your loving brother
write soon   George

Tony Nosis
19423 Klinger
Detroit 12,
Michigan

S. NAVY
JUN 24
430 PM

ADDRESS ONLY   Free

U. S. MARINES WITH PACK HOWITZERS—018

CAMP BLANDING
JUL 18
2 30PM
1944
FLA.

Hello Darling:

Here I am and I'm really tired. Here is a picture of our Island here. We don't see anything like this. We only have sand.

We had our range work and I made Expert the highest possible to make. Army is all right but would rather be home.

Lots of Love. Willy

Pvt. Wm. Hanners 31629
ASN 36983334
Co. D 72nd Bn 69th Reg.
Camp Blanding, Fla.

CAMP BLANDING
2 30PM
1944

POST CARD

PLACE STAMP HERE

NATURAL COLOR POST CARD MADE IN U.S.A. BY E. C. KROPP CO., MILWAUKEE.—(GLL)

U. S. MARINE CORPS PHOTO.

Mr. & Mrs. H. Dykema
48 East Kenilworth Ave.
Villa Park, Ill.

answ'd

Science and the War

The ongoing efforts of the nation's scientific community were instrumental in helping the Allies win the Second World War. The research headed by the Office of Scientific Research and Development gave way to a number of invaluable technological and medical advances that had profound effects on the outcome of the war.

In the country's wars prior to World War II, a great percentage of soldiers died as the result of crude, often septic, surgical instruments and procedures, as well as the lack of proper medication. Wounded soldiers during the Second World War had a much greater chance of survival, particularly due to the availability of the three "miracle" drugs—penicillin, sulfa, and streptomycin. Although penicillin had been discovered by Alexander Fleming more than a decade earlier in England, it was soon to be developed and mass-produced by U.S. pharmaceutical companies, and distributed to the military by 1943. During this time, other advancements in medicine included the development of antihistamines and a vaccine for typhus. Antibiotics in powdered form were also developed and distributed to troops in the field. The powder was sprinkled over wounds to help prevent or minimize infection until further medical treatment was available.

Also significant in saving lives were the establishment of blood banks and the development of new transfusion methods. Furthermore, surgical procedures improved, and more nurses and mobile hospital units served closer to the front lines than in previous wars. The military also established a triage system for assessing the needs of the wounded when medical resources were limited. Those to receive aid first were the ones who were most likely to survive, not those who were most badly wounded.

Intensive scientific research resulted in technological and medical breakthroughs that were critical to the war's outcome.

To reduce the incidence of malaria in certain locations, the government established a number of prevention programs. DDT was used to control mosquito populations, and the drug Atabrine—a quinine substitute—was administered to those who were fighting in malaria-prone areas. Although it did not cure malaria, Atabrine reduced many of its symptoms, allowing soldiers to function until they were able to receive further treatment.

In addition to medical achievements, significant technological advancements tipped the scales in favor of the Allies. Radar, for example, which had been invented by the British in 1932 to detect enemy aircraft, was further developed and utilized during the 1940s. And an improved sonar system made it easier to perceive underwater objects. For detonating anti-aircraft shells from a safe distance, the proximity fuse, which contained a miniature transmitter/receiver, was invented.

Certainly, the most profound scientific advancement of the war came by way of atomic research. In 1905, Albert Einstein's *Special Theory of Relativity* laid the groundwork for the eventual development of atomic weapons. In 1943, the top-secret Manhattan Project was initiated. Through this project, under the leadership of physicist J. Robert Oppenheimer, came the atomic bomb. In August 6, 1945, the first of these bombs, called "Little Boy," was dropped from a B-29 bomber—the *Enola Gay*—on the Japanese city of Hiroshima, killing nearly 70,000. Three days later, a second bomb devastated the city of Nagasaki. Within days, the war was brought to a conclusion with the "unconditional surrender" of Japan.

From the beginning of the conflict to war's end, scientific advancements, both medical and technological, made major contributions to the daily lives of the soldiers and even helped shape the war itself. And these advances would continue to have an impact long after our fighting forces had returned home.

REALISM IN TANK DESTROYER TRAINING,
CAMP HOOD, TEXAS

TROOPS ADVANCING THRU TRENCHES AND
BARB WIRE WHILE LIVE AMMUNITION IS FIRED
DIRECTLY AT THEM, BUT OVERHEAD.

Pvt Thomas H. Tucker 36469165
Co. C. 149th Inf. Rtn. 90th Intr.
Camp Hood Texas

Hi. Bob. Here I am in
the infantry and what
a hole. Bill Crouchman is
here too. How is everything
at the old T. A.? Will write
more later Bye Now
Tucker

23931

FREE

HOOD, TEXAS
JUL 23
1 30 AM
'44

POST CARD

Robert Cummins
Chrysler Tank Arsenal
Dept 99 Paint
Centerline Michigan

PUB. BY BARTON NEWS AGENCY, TEMPLE, TEXAS — NATURAL COLOR POST CARD MADE IN U.S.A. BY E. C. KROPP CO. MILWAUKEE, WIS. (GAM)

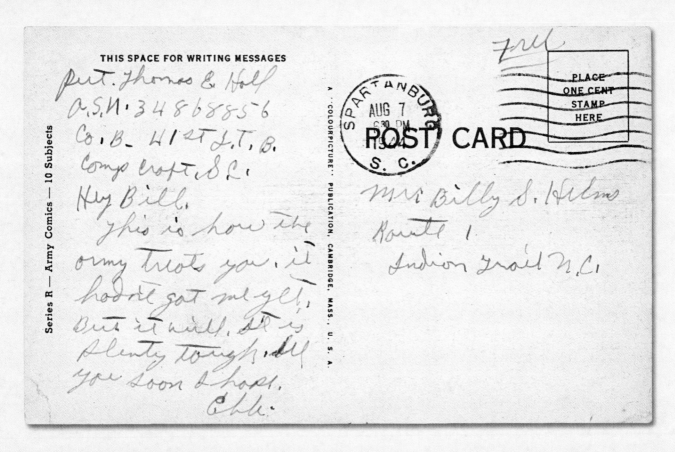

THIS SPACE FOR WRITING MESSAGES

Pvt. Thomas E. Holt
A.S.N. 34868856
Co. B. 41st I.T.B.
Camp Croft, S.C.
Hey Bill.
    This is how the
army treats you. it
hadn't got me yet,
But it will. It is
Plenty tough. See
you soon I hope.
            Chb.

Series R — Army Comics — 10 Subjects

A "COLOURPICTURE" PUBLICATION, CAMBRIDGE, MASS., U.S.A.

SPARTANBURG
AUG 7
6 30 PM
1944
S. C.

POST CARD

PLACE
ONE CENT
STAMP
HERE

Mr. Billy S. Helms
Route 1
Indian Trail N.C.

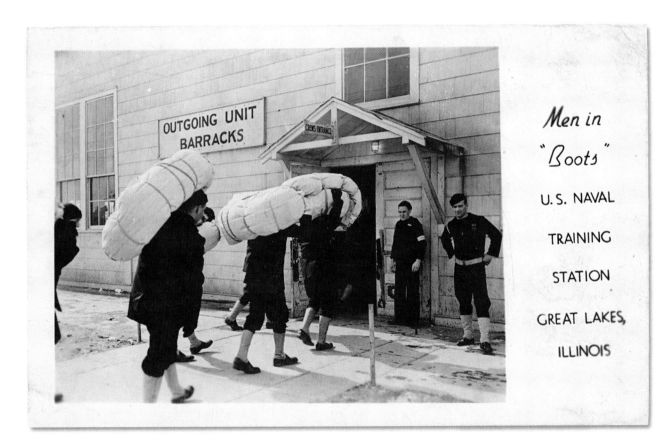

OUTGOING UNIT BARRACKS

CHIEF'S ENTRANCE

Men in "Boots"
U.S. NAVAL
TRAINING
STATION
GREAT LAKES,
ILLINOIS

9/26/44

Hi
  Arrived at
10:30 A.M. the food
stinks and so does
the Navy. Not much
choice. After "Boot"
you either get sea or
sub service. Nothing
else to write.
        Love Bruce
Russell B. Brown A.S.
Co 1868 U.S.N.T.C.
Great Lakes Ill.
    U. S. Navy.

C.T. ARMY COMICS

GENUINE CURTEICH-CHICAGO "C.T. ART-COLORTONE" POST CARD (REG. U.S. PAT. OFF.)

GREAT LAKE
SEP 27
5 AM
1944
ILL.

POST CARD

PLACE
ONE CENT
STAMP
HERE

Norma Duplaga.
3757 W 116.
  Cleve. Ohio.

PVT ARTHUR MICHELS
1ST RC. B-01A
1222 REC. SC SC
CAMP UPTON N.Y.

Dear Mother:

By the time I get this I will be on my merry way. I do not know where but will let you know when I do will you telegraph me a little money as I am flat as of the present moment. lovingly Arthur

POST CARD

MR & MRS LEO V. MICHELS
138 JEROME AVE
MINEOLA, N.Y.

CAMP UPTON
NOV 28
3 10 PM
1942
N.Y.

PLACE
ONE CENT
STAMP
HERE
2B-H721

GENUINE CURTEICH-CHICAGO "C.T. ART-COLORTONE" POST CARD (REG. U.S. PAT. OFF.)

C. T. ART COLORS

USO
Cœur d'Alene Idaho

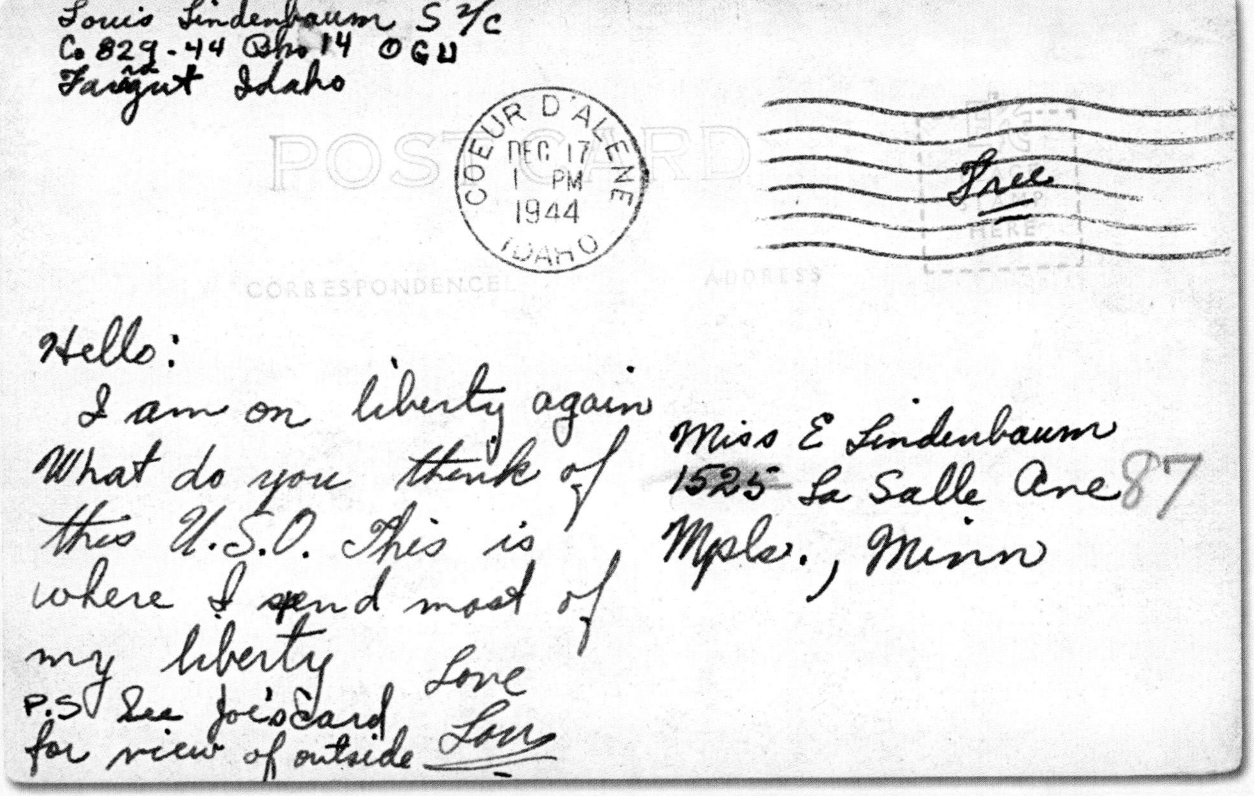

Louis Lindenbaum S2/c
Co 829-44 Bn 14 OGU
Fargut Idaho

COEUR D'ALENE
DEC 17
1 PM
1944
IDAHO

POSTCARD

CORRESPONDENCE

ADDRESS

Free

Hello:
    I am on liberty again
What do you think of
this U.S.O. This is
where I spend most of
my liberty
P.S See Joe's card   Love
for view of outside   Lou

Miss E Lindenbaum
1525 La Salle Ave 87
Mpls., Minn

1945

Since 1941, the bulk of America's wartime effort had been dedicated to winning the European war. Early in 1945, it was apparent that the once unstoppable Nazi juggernaut had crumbled under the weight of Allied assault. In January, the Soviets had taken Warsaw and liberated Auschwitz, and the Germans had withdrawn from the Ardennes. In early February, Stalin, Churchill, and Roosevelt met at Yalta—their second "Big Three" summit—where they discussed the defeat of Germany and the shape of postwar Europe. In early April, German armies in the Ruhr surrendered, marking the end of organized resistance outside Berlin. In the weeks that followed, American forces were able to make their way through Austria, Czechoslovakia, and Germany unopposed.

On April 12, the joy of imminent victory was marred by the sudden death of President Roosevelt, who suffered a cerebral hemorrhage. As the nation mourned the loss of one leader, Harry S. Truman was sworn in as President, and it was he who would bring the war to a close. At the end of April, as the Red Army occupied Berlin, a defeated Hitler committed suicide, and only days later, on May 7, German General Alfred Jodl surrendered unconditionally.

Truman and Churchill triumphantly declared May 8 as Victory in Europe (V-E) Day.

Allied attention now turned to the Pacific, where the war was still being fought with Japan. In February, American marines had taken Iwo Jima, the most costly battle of the Pacific war, and leapt into Okinawa two months later. As the nation geared up for the invasion of Japan itself, technology made it unnecessary. On August 6, the *Enola Gay,* an American B-29 bomber, flew over Japan and dropped a single atomic bomb on Hiroshima, devastating the city. On August 9, a second bomb was dropped on Nagasaki. A shattered Japan surrendered on August 14, and Americans joyfully celebrated Victory over Japan (V-J) Day.

The war was finally over, an event that precipitated delirious worldwide happiness. In the United States, singing people took to the streets, car horns blared, hats were tossed high into the air, and shredded bits of paper showered down from open windows. People laughed and cheered; total strangers hugged and kissed one another. Sirens and factory whistles and church bells added to the delirium. Peace had been achieved, but at a tremendous cost. Over 60 million soldiers from twenty-six Allied nations and three Axis powers had fought, 50 million lives were lost, and both Europe and Asia were devastated.

Although the war had not been waged on American soil, the country's face had been altered. Conventional prewar gender and racial standards had changed and would continue to evolve. In 1945, approximately 19 million women held jobs that were once filled by men, and although many returned to their traditional roles, others maintained their places in the workforce. During the war, the number of both marriages and divorces had increased tremendously, and the transition to peacetime living was certain to be challenging. One fact was sure, the pent-up buying power of the American people would be unleashed by peace, and the years after 1945 would see an unparalleled economic boom. Birth rates would soar, suburbia would be created, and the automobile would become a necessity of life. In time, the frozen dinner—a timesaver for the homemaker—was developed to serve the new world. In 1945, famous science fiction author Arthur C. Clarke came up with the concept of using satellites to transmit information, an idea soon to become a reality.

The year 1945 saw the conclusion to what many consider the most important event in the history of the United States. The country emerged from the war a newly industrialized nation, characterized by a robust economy and a military force of unparalleled might. Strong and victorious, a transformed nation with eyes forward, now focused its energy on the building of a secure future. ✎

A moment frozen in time . . .
News of the war's conclusion was met
with joyous worldwide celebration.

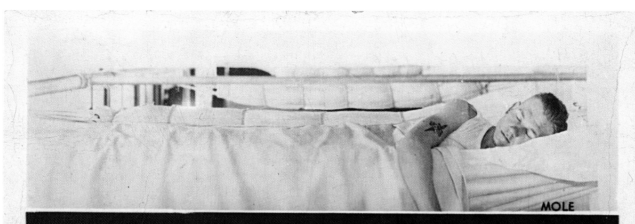

MOLE

A SAILOR'S PRAYER

NOW I LAY ME DOWN TO SLEEP
I PRAY THE LORD MY SOUL TO KEEP;
GRANT NO OTHER SAILOR TAKE
MY SHOES AND SOCKS BEFORE I WAKE;
LORD, GUARD ME IN MY SLUMBER
AND KEEP MY HAMMOCK ON ITS NUMBER;
MAY NO CLUES NOR LASHINGS BREAK
AND LET ME DOWN, BEFORE I WAKE.
KEEP ME SAFELY IN THY SIGHT
AND GRANT NO FIRE DRILL TONIGHT;
AND IN THE MORNING LET ME WAKE
BREATHING SCENTS OF SIRLOIN STEAK.
GOD PROTECT ME IN MY DREAMS
AND MAKE THIS BETTER THAN IT SEEMS.

GRANT THE TIME MAY SWIFTLY FLY
WHEN MYSELF SHALL REST ON HIGH.
IN A SNOWY FEATHER BED
WHERE I LONG TO REST MY HEAD
FAR AWAY FROM ALL THESE SCENES
AND THE SMELL OF HALF DONE BEANS.
TAKE ME BACK INTO THE LAND
WHERE THEY DON'T SCRUB DOWN WITH SAND;
WHERE NO DEMON TYPHOON BLOWS
WHERE THE WOMEN WASH THE CLOTHES;
GOD THOU KNOWEST ALL MY WOES —
FEED ME IN MY DYING THROES;
TAKE ME BACK I'LL PROMISE THEN
NEVER TO LEAVE HOME AGAIN...

★ FOUR YEARS LATER ★

OUR FATHER WHO ART IN WASHINGTON
PLEASE, DEAR FATHER, LET ME STAY
DO NOT DRIVE ME NOW AWAY
WIPE AWAY MY SCALDING TEARS
AND LET ME STAY FOR THIRTY YEARS
PLEASE FORGIVE ME ALL MY PAST
AND THINGS THAT HAPPENED
    AT THE MAST
DO NOT MY REQUEST REFUSE
AND LET ME STAY ANOTHER CRUISE.

GEORGE HUBLEY S1/C
U.S.N.T.C. — Co. 148
GREAT LAKES, ILL.

DEAR LEMON AND HELEN:
    YOU CAN THANK
GOD EVERY NITE
YOU STILL HAVE
CIVILIAN CLOTHES.

FREE

MR. AND MRS. LAMAR LEHR
137 N. NEWBERRY ST.
    YORK, PENNA.

Mess Hall
U.S. NAVAL TRAINING CENTER, GREAT LAKES, ILLINOIS

Donald Eugene Neerken A.S.
Company 613 U.S.N.T.C.
Great Lakes Ill.

POST CARD

GREAT LAKES
MAY 3
7³⁰ AM
1945
ILL

Free
STAMP
HERE

CORRESPONDENCE

ADDRESS

GROGAN PHOTO—DANVILLE, ILLINOIS

Dear Folks;
    Well here's our
mess hall, but don't
look for me. I haven't
my uniform as yet.
You'll probably get
my Civilian clothes in
a couple of day's. Will
write more later. Your
                        Son
                        Don.

Mr & Mrs. A. Neerken
75 Fayette Street
Grandville,
        Michigan

"We build, we fight."
Seabees—naval construction battalions
that enlisted over 350,000 workers—
built bridges, warehouses, hundreds
of airstrips, and thousands of miles of
roads in every battle zone.

No. 1659   Obstacle Course—Camp Endicott, R. I.
Official U. S. Navy Photo

Gun Crew in Victory Formation

OFFICIAL U. S. NAVY PHOTOGRAPH

"Man your battle stations!"
To be ready for battle at a moment's
notice, a gunner's crew diligently
trained every day to perfect the
coordination of each man's special job,
including the communication
of orders and the loading and
aiming of weapons.

P.S. I can't hardly open
my mouth

THIS SPACE FOR WRITING MESSAGES

Dear Mom & Dad.
Well I am writ-
ing a card
I didn't feel
like writing. I
had two teeth
pulled out today
and they don't feel
too good. He pulled
them in two 2 seconds.
I just had a half a
pint of Ice Cream.
Will write tommorow
Love. Buddy.

Harold L. Shumen a/s
Co. 160 Unit C-9
U. S. N. T. C.
Sampson N.Y.

FREE

PLACE
ONE CENT
STAMP
HERE

POST CARD

A COLOURPICTURE PUBLICATION, CAMBRIDGE, MASS. U. S. A.

Mr. & Mrs. Alphus Shumen

Honesdale R.D. 4

Penna.

Going Home

The atomic bombs that exploded over Hiroshima and Nagasaki in August 1945, signaled the end of the greatest conflict in world history. For the 12 million Americans still on active duty, the explosions meant that they would soon be going home. When Washington's planning for the greatest demobilization in American history began in 1943, emphasis was on speed rather than efficiency. The War Department decided that a citizen's leaving the service would occur as it had begun—as individuals. Unlike the Grand Review parades that had marked the end of the Civil War, there would be no final viewing of the armies. Although a poll taken among soldiers in 1944 showed that fully 75 percent believed that two years of service merited an immediate discharge, demobilization criteria for each veteran would be based instead on the number of "points" he had accumulated during service. These points were based on length of time served, amount of time spent overseas, combat experience, and size of individual families.

After V-E Day, the Army and the Air Corps began to apply the demobilization plan to the forces that had defeated the Nazis. It was a matter of supreme indifference to the GIs that the most capable and experienced soldiers were the same ones who were most eligible for demobilization. Longest in service, combat-tested soldiers would go home, and new recruits would fill their place in the ranks. The unit may have been destined for the invasion of Japan, but its efficiency was certain to be affected. Soldiers simply wanted out and carefully counted the points that would bring them home. Veterans got one point for each month of service, five points for every campaign ribbon or wound received, and twelve points for each of their children. Multitudes without "good-bye babies" complained they had been denied the chance to propagate. Regardless of opportunity or performance, it took a total of eighty-five points to merit discharge. By June, the process had gotten underway.

WESTERN UNION

CLASS OF SERVICE

This is a full-rate Telegram or Cablegram unless its deferred character is indicated by a suitable symbol above or preceding the address.

A. N. WILLIAMS
PRESIDENT

NEWCOMB CARLTON
CHAIRMAN OF THE BOARD

J. C. WILLEVER
FIRST VICE-PRESIDENT

SYMBOLS
DL=Day Letter
NT=Overnight Telegram
LC=Deferred Cable
NLT=Cable Night Letter
Ship Radiogram

The filing time shown in the date line on telegrams and day letters is STANDARD TIME at point of origin. Time of receipt is STANDARD TIME at point of destination

NBE110 20=WUX FORTMCDOWELL CALIF OCT 4 1037A

1945 OCT 4 PM 5 39

MISS ROSLYN BERGENFELD=

CARE D STEIN 11 HILLSIDE AVE=

=ARRIVED SAFELY FEELING FINE. LET MORRIS KNOW. WILL PHONE AS
SOON AS I CAN. ALL MY LOVE TO YOU DARLING=

MAC.

333P.

Y WILL APPRECIATE SUGGESTIONS FROM

After V-J Day, the total points needed for demobilization fell to eighty. No invasion of Japan was necessary, and in October, the points were further reduced to sixty. But for those who were anxiously awaiting the return of their loved ones, the process could not be fast enough. There was intense pressure on Congress and the War Department to "get the boys home." Planes and ships were quickly mobilized for their transport.

The Army had 8.3 million men under arms in May, but only 4.1 million at the end of December. President Harry S. Truman, alarmed at the hollowing-out of the American armed strength just as the Cold War was beginning, asked Congress to approve the system of Universal Military Training (UMT). His recommendation was ignored. Instead, on January 1, 1946, the magic number for going home was further reduced to only fifty points. By June, the army that had defeated fascism numbered only 2 million.

The postwar demobilization process, driven by political expediency rather than long-range need, proved to be inefficient and wasteful. Not only

were the most highly trained veterans in every service permitted to leave, but also millions of dollars worth of equipment was abandoned; veterans said they permitted it to "Rust in Place" (RIP). But in a larger sense, the process suited the American wartime experience. Millions of civilians were drafted; they combined with the nation's industrial might to build the greatest military force in history; and after victory, they demanded an immediate return home. Although the draft continued until 1973, the Cold War would be fought by a different American military.

1821—Marines Swarm Ashore.

10 June 45.

1821—Marines are shown in amphibious operations. These marines are landing from several types of amphibious craft, in background. Training for this kind of action is given at the Amphibious Training Base at Fort Pierce, Florida.
—Official U. S. Navy Photo

POST CARD

THIS SPACE FOR ADDRESS ONLY

Free USN

Dear Sis,

Sorry I haven't written sooner but I've been awfully busy and haven't had much time to write.

We have a 48 today but I'm broke as usual so didn't go off the base. I'll try to write you a letter soon. I'm going swiming now.

Mrs. Dorothy Haffenden
R#5 Box 238
Battle Creek
Michigan.

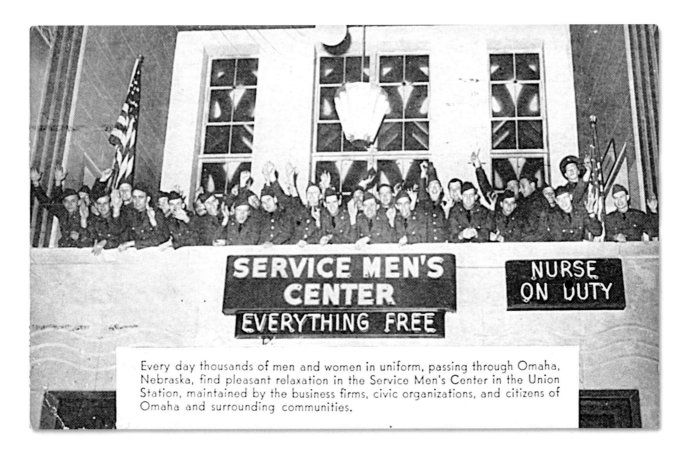

SERVICE MEN'S CENTER
EVERYTHING FREE

NURSE ON DUTY

Every day thousands of men and women in uniform, passing through Omaha, Nebraska, find pleasant relaxation in the Service Men's Center in the Union Station, maintained by the business firms, civic organizations, and citizens of Omaha and surrounding communities.

Dear Mom & Pops.

If Dick calls I know you will be nice to him as no doubt he will some day be your son-in-law, when I get over the sharp memories of the Past; & when we are both out of the Service. I didn't have time to ask you if you like him or not.

How about it?

Write soon Love M.L.

Pvt. M.L. Henry 1761758)
Sq W 426 A.A.T. B.U. (Free
Mountain Home Idaho.

Mrs M.E. Crandall
254 Oneita St.
Battle Creek, Mich.

UNION PACIFIC RAILROAD COMPANY, OMAHA, NEBRASKA

Post Card

GIs brought home almost 100,000 "war brides" in 1945.

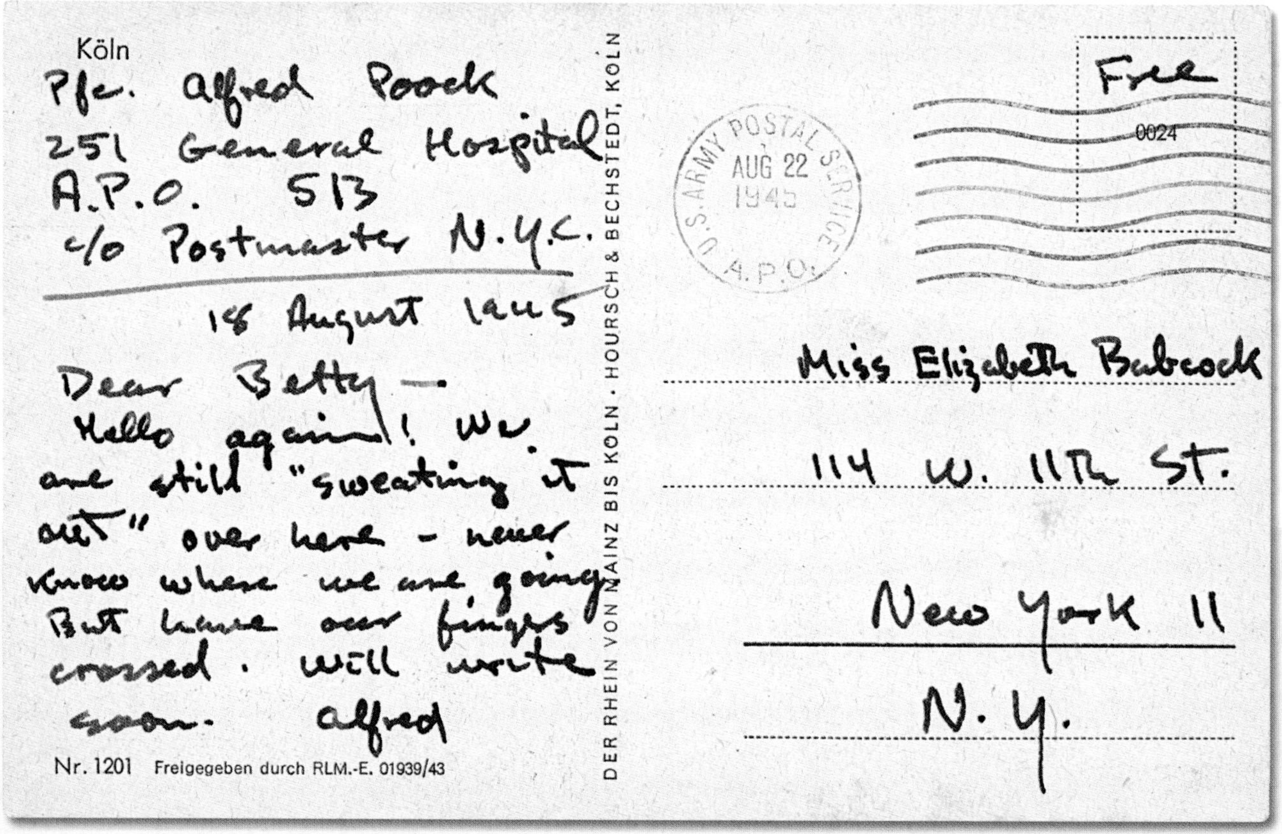

Köln

Pfc. Alfred Poock
251 General Hospital
A.P.O. 513
c/o Postmaster N.Y.C.

18 August 1945

Dear Betty —

Hello again! We
are still "sweating it
out" over here - never
know where we are going.
But have our fingers
crossed. Will write
soon. Alfred

Nr. 1201 Freigegeben durch RLM.-E. 01939/43

DER RHEIN VON MAINZ BIS KÖLN · HOURSCH & BECHSTEDT, KÖLN

U.S. ARMY POSTAL SERVICE
AUG 22 1945
A.P.O.

Free
0024

Miss Elizabeth Babcock

114 W. 11th St.

New York 11

N.Y.

Re. C 3   Chapel—Reception Center, Fort Dix, N. J.

337 Fairview Ave.
Waynesboro, Pa.

Aug. 25, 1945

POST CARD

THIS SPACE FOR ADDRESS ONLY   FREE

Dear Janet,
        Ho! Hum! I've been
here a week yesterday &
still havent heard anything.
We cant get any passes so
were just "stuck" till they
decide what the score is.
If they would bring those points
down I might have a chance
to get out. I'm still hoping I'll
get to see you before you leave
for college. I wont be shipped over
again, like you said. Thanks Ha! Ha!
    Take it easy.   Love, Lloyd

Miss Janet Good

Phila. Ave.

Waynesboro,

Penna.

1264 Fliegeraufnahme Schwabinger Krankenhaus

Love to my Darling Wife

98th General Hospital
Oct 11 1945 Munich
Germany

Here I lye in my little
bed thinking of You dear.
some times I get up & roam
the halls & talk to my
self. Just Wishing I was
home to talking to you
Dear. but a long ways
a part. my love; but some
day my Wish may come
true, With love Your
Darling Husband.

Lin, Ord

Sgt Seaton

Conclusion

In the same way that members of a future generation would remember where they were when they learned that President John F. Kennedy was assassinated, people who were alive on December 7, 1941, would forever recall where they were upon hearing the news of Pearl Harbor. World War II itself served as the defining point in the lives of millions of Americans—an event that truly unified the nation. The war was considered a personal crusade in the eyes of the country's sons and daughters, who rallied behind it with an intense spirit of self-sacrifice. Never before or since has a conflict, believed to be necessary for the preservation of moral goodness and decency throughout the world, been met with such overwhelming public support.

Pride in winning the war would be forever mixed with grief over those who had given their lives for peace. The nation would continue to honor its fallen heroes, and time would burnish the civil efforts that supported the conflict. All of the endeavors of the wartime generation are worthy of our attention. If *Postcards from World War II* helps us recapture the triumphs and the tragedies of that time, it will have served its purpose.

"This is a solemn but a glorious hour. I only wish that Franklin D. Roosevelt had lived to witness this day. General Eisenhower informs me that the forces of Germany have surrendered to the United Nations. The flags of freedom fly over all Europe. . . . I call upon the people of the United States, whatever their faith, to unite in offering joyful thanks to God for the victory we have won, and to pray that He will support us to the end of our present struggle and guide us into the ways of peace. I also call upon my countrymen to dedicate the day of prayer to the memory of those who have given their lives to make possible our victory."

Harry S. Truman
Broadcast to American People
following surrender of Germany.
May 8, 1945

For the purpose of clarity, each of the handwritten messages found on the postcards have been transcribed and appear below. Minimal clarifications have been made, and are denoted by brackets.

1941

Page 8. Hello "Speed," I arrived here all in decent shape and progressing thru the course qui[te] steadily. Not much practical work but intend to start next wk sometime. Tell Clyde, Ed, and Squeak to write besides yourself when answering. Would have wrote sooner but been studying hard and etc. Are you still going to B.C. and Albion roller skating, as yet, and getting charlies horses Ha!Ha! Us fellows from Custer here for this school all say hello and write. Save this card for me will you because I want to give it to Esther my girl friend. / Your old room pal, Al

Page 10. Dear Mother & Dad, Here I am in the U.S. Army, & so far its not too bad. Don't know how long I'll be here--probably just a few days & then again it might be a few months. They don't tell you very much here, so you have to find out for yourself or not at all. Food here is very good for Army life--we do have beans, but also other things. Had watermelon for lunch.

Been busy all day & am going to shave & go to bed. Will write later. Let Grandma & the rest know where I am for now. Don't send anything here for awhile, ouside of a letter or so because I may be moved & may not get it. / Love, Son, Edwin

Page 12. Hello Jigs, Well they got me in the army now, and its not bad. They are going to make a pil[l] pusher out of me. Im in the 26th Battalion of a medical training center Co A. Bldg.308. Camp Grant, Ill. It took me a long time to write but I thought that you might want to know where I am. / Pal George

Page 14. Hi Boys, See if you can get me an advance on my 1942 salary. Has Red got those valve stem guides done yet? I met Bob Bachman at Camp Grant, Ill. (under a table) & Oscar Getcine here in Texas. Having fine time. Wish I was there. Tell "Tis" & Red to write. / "Red"

Page 18. Hello – Just a line or two – will write later – Thanks for lovely cookie & stamps & medal – sho was swell / Love, Fritz Blair

Page 20. 12/1/41 - Hi Ed: Been working like a beaver the last two days. Was taken from a detail this afternoon. Filled out a bunch of discharge papers, seen my Service Records. Discharge date stamped on them is Dec-14-41. I'll be seeing you about Christmas. / Stanley

1942

Page 24. Hi Honey, This is just about how it looks at night when all the planes are ready. Hope you like the cards. I have some more but I will send them later. I think I will write a few lines to my bro Chuck and to your bro Jimmey so I will close. With all my Love to the sweetest wife in the world. / Your Hubby Leroy xxxxxxxxxxxxxxxxx

Page 26. Hi Neighbor, Please forgive me for not writing for so long a period of time, but you see we're pretty busy through the day now and New York City is so attractive at night that I can hardly stay away from it. I'm now at Fort Hamilton - Brooklyn waiting to be shipped out. Where we will go or when we will leave I don't know, but as far as I'm concerned they can leave me here for the duration. This New York is O.K. Please forgive the old post card, but it was all I had to write on. / Sincerely Charlie

Page 28. Hello Folks: Just came from Camp Robinson Ark. Am on an inspection tour of army vehicles for the second army. My new home will be in Camp Tyson - Paris Tenn. when I get back to my company. Came through a tough snow blizzard in the Ozark Mts. / Carl

Page 32. Dear Loveones; Just a line to let you know I am O.K. only longing to see you all. Sure hope you all are the same, dear loveones. Here is a picture of one of our tanks. Would you like to take a ride in it? Sure do make a noise, when they pass you on the road. There sure is lots of guns on them too. It will sure mow those Germans down when we get over there, won't it? There is 4 men in one of them. Well, I will close, and write a letter tomorrow. Ans. soon. / Watson

Page 34. Hello Minerva- Sorry I couldn't answer sooner but was pretty busy. I've moved to a flying school now so when the weather permits we fly 6 days a week. The weather is usually warm & dry but the last 3 days we've had rain so we're grounded. I'll write more later. / Yours, Larry R.

Page 36. Hi Gwen, Do you look like this in your grass skirt dear? So far I haven't seen anyone that does. Don't forget the picture. Love, Bob

Page 38. Dear Palsy: I'm going to machinist school here for the next 18 weeks. Its nice here and a guy can learn a lot. Here's where you should be. You could be a _greese_ ball. Tell Bill and your Mom and folks Hello and don't forget to write me that letter this time. / Your Pal, Leo

Page 40. _Dearest_ _Betty_. Thought this was pretty so got it especially for you. It finally cleared up here and now there are no clouds in sight. This [is] a lot prettier than Camp Wolters was. I miss the gang though and above all I miss _you_. So keep praying, Angel, for our dreams to come true and our prayers to be answered. / Always Your Benny

Page 42. Dear Son, Glad to hear you can drive the car so good - hope you feel good - be nice to Mother, you will be well paid - how is sandy, rabbits and all the chickens - hows the garden - I suppose you will be going to school soon / From Daddy

Page 44. Dear Wife, I wait for your letters so write me every day. I am lonesome without you. I love you and think of you all the time. / Your Dear Husband Charles

Page 46. Hi Diann. Whats the matter are your hands cut off & haven't learned to write with your feet yet? I've been waiting for a letter from you. I've answered your letter as near as I can remember. Hope your in the best of health & so on. I'm feeling great. Hoping to get a letter soon. I must close. / As Ever, Pvt. John H. Merljur

Page 48. Hi Pal: Are you dead? Then why don't you drop a line to me? If things pan out I might see you during the holidays. Best regards to all. / Will

Page 52. *Hello you Big Polock, How is everything up there? Im getting along OK. This place Im at now seems to be the last place at the end of the world. How is Sherman making out in the army thing. Haven't sent him across yet have they. I guess there is where most of us will be before long. They told us down here by the middle of next summer 75% of us would be in foreign service. The way I hear I guess there aint many of the fellows left anymore up home. / (Jinks) / P.S. Please write and let me know how you are.*

Page 54. *Hello Slim, Am having a swell time here and am getting ready to be shipped out of this camp soon. Say "Hello" to Steve & Robert and tell them both to enlist now as they need a couple of Generals. I like everything about the army except this thing they call K.P. and they lay it on thick. I'll write a letter as soon as I get in a permanent camp. / Johnny*

Page 56. *Dear Friend: This is a H____ of a climate, we have seen the sun 3 times, on a clear day we see this same view. Lets hear from you. / Walter*

Page 58. *Dear Children: I hope you are having a Merry Christmas today with out your daddy at home. Write and let me know what Santa brought you. / Love from Daddy*

Page 60. *Hello Honey, I am sorry I can't write because of duty - keeps me busy. I'll explain when I see you. You can start preparing our wedding because I will be shipped near here. I love you very much. See you first chance I get time to hi[t]ch hike home. / Love Phil*

1943

Page 64. *Dear Ma, I got the stamps - for which thanks. I'm still waiting for my swim suit. I'll let you know as soon as I get it. Can you find me on the other side of the card? Don't look too hard because I'm not on there! See the kind of barracks we live in? No stoves now! / Mick*

Page 66. *Dear Miriam & Eli, Got in yesterday afternoon – the place is a Paradise. They kill you with kindness etc. Brick buildings, steam & stuff. No restrictions, no fuss, no nuthin — More in the next note. Keep em smiling. Regards to all at the U.S.O. / Murray*

Page 68. *Hi Folks, I am fine & well. Just a card & few lines. I drove today on range & drive a 4,000 gal tank of gasoline. What a job. I love it. Grant [w]rote on Thurs. & Skip on Fri. It's warm today & beautiful out. More later — / Love Pvt. Leo Clark xx*

Page 70. *Hello Baby, I hope your not mad yet. You see this girl wants to help out?? I love you. / Phil*

Page 72. *I am quite busy with tests. I have to go on guard duty from 1:00 to 3:00 in the Morning. We had a hurricane here and had to have 4 men to hold down each tent. No one was hurt. Along with the wind we had rain and all of our things got wet. The weather is getting warm so by tomorrow our cloth[es] will be dry. Write. / Pvt Wesley Hanke*

Page 74. *Dear Darling Wife, Have you been getting my letters. Haven't heard from you lately. Please write soon. I am writing a nice letter this morning. I got to go on guard mount Thursday. / Your Husband Marty / I love you Dear always*

Page 76. *Hi Jim, sorry I couldn't talk longer on the phone but I will call some other time. How is Daisy? It is raining here. The picture is natural around here. Those jeeps hit a bump & jump about 6 ft into the air. Well so long for now. / Larry*

Page 78. *Hello my darling Wife. Just a seasons greetings to you. Please dear try and enjoy yourself for the holidays. Give my love to the family too. I am fine, and in the best of health. I hope you are getting mail from me. I am always yours forever. / Love Phil*

Page 80. *Hellow Neighbor, I am well & hope you are all the same. Its been warm here & there is one thing that is really funny about this place. you sweat like heck in the sun but when you sit in the shade of a tree you dog-gone near freeze. believe me that is the truth. If there is any news of back home please tell me about it. / Your good friend & neighbor, Pvt Nicholas*

Page 82. *Hi Elda, I wonder if you'll still be in Cleveland when this gets there. Are you going to keep the canteen open at all during the summer? If not, how about sending me your home address, so that I can reform, and write to you now and then. How did you make out in your course? At least a B, I'll bet. / Johnny*

Page 84. *Hi Dad: How are you getting along? Is the corn up yet? I bet the wheat looks nice by now. Do you have any more fresh cows? Try and write me. / Eddie*

Page 86. *Brad: These are the type of planes I'll be training in several weeks when I get to Advanced. Pre-Flight is nearing it's close now and I'm doing swell. Give my regards to Elaine and the boys of #324. / Bob*

Page 88. *Dear Mom: Have been working sort of hard of late and have neglected all my correspondence--June especially. Of course the local belles have provided some time consumin[g] diversion--that is what time there didst exist. I have my work caught up for approximately three months now . . . hope they don't change jobs on me as I like this one. Of course, the daily routines and jobs that arise will need my attention. I sent June nothing on*

her birthday the 26. She'll annihilate me - I betja. My last information was to the fact that Lowell's marriage had been postponed indefinitely else I might have showed up. Sorry I missed it. / CH Allen

Page 90. *Dear Alice: I haven't heard from you this week. Is there anything wrong? I got [an]other shot in my arm today. Boy! Is it killing me. I am going to sleep now. With Love, a good night to you. / Mike*

Page 92. *Dear Lydia, Would have written sooner but am quite busy. A hailstorm destroyed my V garden. I am O.K. just a little lonesome. Sure is hot out here. Sure like the papers. Thanks. Hope your folks are all O.K. / Love "Bill"*

Page 94. *Hi Pal, How's everything with you. I got my uniform. I'll be leaving for camp soon. I'll write sooner. Good Luck / Pal Nick*

Page 96. *Dear Mil: Sure hope we get these orders soon. I _ _ _ _ this place. /Don*

Page 100. *Dear Mil: This is a platform that the fellows have to leap off before they pass you here. It is to practice abandoning ship. / "Don"*

Page 102. *Dear Mil: Don't give a D_ _ _ if I never get close enough to do this. I would rather be in the Home Guards. / Love Don*

Page 104. *Dear Mother & Dad, I am OK but kinda lonesome. So drop me a line now and then. Hope you are both OK. When you write use the address at the top of the card. / Love from your son Jim*

Page 106. *Hello Jerk, Feeling fine Steve. Getting my furlogh on this week or next for sure. Getting married on my furlogh. Bertie getting married on 26th of Oct. Chuckie is my usher. Don't forget to come Steve. I['ll] be waiting. / Your Pal Johnny*

Page 108. *Hello Lloyd; Having a good time working day [and] nite. I'm in charge of the mess-hall now. Hope you are well and getting along alright. No rationing on liquors out this way. Come on out. / Your Bro. Glenn J. Lewis*

Page 110. *This is our menu. I didn't eat very much. I wasn't very hungry. I am going to go to the canteen with Weier. / Carl*

1944

Page 114. *Dear Folks, I got here about four o'clock this morning. I was four hours late. Don't expect to be here long. I am living in a tent. Dolly and I didn't get married. It is raining out here. I will tell you more when I write a letter. / Love Harvey*

Page 116. *Shellac costs $11.00 a bottle down here. How many cases do you want. Frank & Thelma look swell but Frank lost eight lbs. But feels good now. Boy were they glad to see me. They are staying at a swell home. / Uncle Bitz*

Page 118. *Hi Ma, This card is just off the serious side. I took my classification tests yesterday and got all high marks. Way above average. They want to make me a radioman but you have to have three years of typing which I haven't had. Will write later. / Andy*

Page 120. *Hello Folks – How's the world treating you by this time? I hope your all in good shape. I am OK, but give me <u>home</u> any old time. We're keeping pretty busy down here. But the chow is pretty good. / Your Bro-in-law, Clark, Jr.*

Page 126. *Just received you letter today and also the 2 (you know what I mean). You don't have to worry about my coming home because the train fare to boston is taken out of your pay and the tickets bought for you so you can expect me anytime the last week of this month. See you soon / Andy*

Page 128. *Hi Folks: Believe it or not I'm the "POP" of all the Marine Recruits here on the "Island" and don't think for a minute I don't feel like it. What a setup. Tomorrow is our first 20 mile hike. I'm looking forward to falling out and getting a ride back to the barracks. Regards to all / Ralph*

Page 130. *Dear Richie & Lesily, Here is an S.N.J navy scout trainer plane. I am very sorry I couldn't talk to you on the phone, but I am going to call again at your house. And early to. I sure do miss you Richie. Don't forget me now. Love Merle & Dick xoxoxox*

Page 132. *Have arrived here Sunday and was surprised to see the terrific change taken place in my son. He is ill from worry and hates to be here. All boys that came in with him are gone about a week already. / Mrs. A. Oliver Olejack*

Page 134. *Hi Tony, How is the old man getting along. I hope you are all right. Over here I'm just fine. Tell ma that's me on the other side. Tony don't enlist in anything please. I am sorry myself so do me that favor OK. I'll write you a letter when I have time. So long for now. / Your Loving brother George / P.S. Write Soon.*

Page 136. *Hello Darling: Here I am and I'm really tired. Here is a picture of our land here. We don't see anything like this. We only have sand. We had our range work and I made Expert, the highest possible to make. Army is all right but would rather be home. / Lots of Love, Willy*

Page 138. *Hi Bob, Here I am in the infantry and what a hole. Bill*

Crouchman is here too. How is everything at the old T.A.? Will write more later. / Bye Now, Tucker

Page 142. Hey Bill, This is how the army treats you. It hasn't got me yet, but it will. It is plenty tough. See you soon I hope / Eble.

Page 144. Hi, Arrived safe at 10:30 A.M. The food stinks and so does the Navy. Not much choice. After "Boot" you either get sea or sub service. Nothing else to write. / Love Bruce

Page 146. Dear Mother: By the time [you] get this, I will be on my merry way. I do not know where but will let you know when I do. Will you telegraph me a little money as I am flat as of the present moment. / Lovingly, Arty

Page 148. Hello: I am on liberty again. What do you think of this U.S.O. This is where I spend most of my liberty / Love Lou / P.S. See Joe's card for view of outside

1945

Page 152. Dear Lemon and Helen: You can thank God every nite you still have civilian clothes.

Page 154. Dear Folks; Well here's our mess hall, but don't look for me. I haven't my uniform as yet. You'll probably get my Civilian clothes in a couple of day's. Will write more later. / Your Son Don

Page 156. Dear Pat, How are you. This is what we have to do here. If you don't write me I am going to quit writing you. This is the second card I have written you. Be a good girl and help mom. / Love, Daddy

Page 158. Dear Mom & Dad: Well I am sending a card because I didn't feel much like writing. I had two teeth pulled out today and they don't feel too good. He pulled them in two 2 seconds. I just had a half a pint of ice cream. Will write tommorrow. / Love, Lindy / P.S. I can't hardly open my mouth.

Page 162. Dear Sis, Sorry I haven't written sooner but I've been awfully busy and haven't had much time to write. We have a 48 today but I'm broke as usual, so didn't go off the base. I'll try to write you a letter soon. I'm going swimming now. / Love Brooks

Page 164. Dear Mom & Pops - If Dick calls I hope you will be nice to him as no doubt he will someday be your son-in-law, when I get over the sharp memories of the past, & when we are both out of the Service. I didn't have time to ask you if you like him or not. How about it? Write soon. / Love, M.L.

Page 166. Dear Betty – Hello again! We are still "sweating it out" over here – never know where we are going. But have our fingers crossed. Will write soon. / Alfred

Page 168. Dear Janet, Ho! Hum! I've been here a week yesterday & still havent heard anything. We cant get any passes so were just "stuck" till they decide what the score is. If they would bring those points down I might have a chance to get out. I'm still hoping I'll get to see you before you leave for college. I won't be shipped over again, like you said. Thanks, Ha! Ha! Take it easy. / Love, Lloyd

Page 170. 98th General Hospital - Here I lye in my little bed thinking of you dear. Sometimes I get up & roam the halls & talk to myself. Just wishing I was home talking to you dear. But a long ways apart my love; but some day my wish may come true. With love, your darling husband, Linford

All numbers that appear in blue type indicate pages that include postcard images.

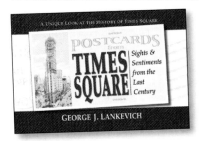
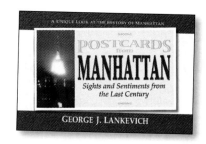
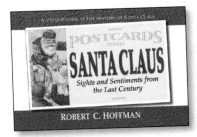